MW01105811

Five Thimbles

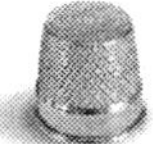 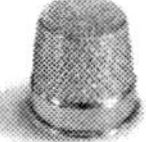 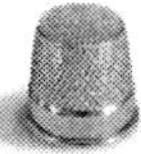  

A Tennessee childhood memoir

Paula Grizzell DeMarini

The stories in this book are true. Understanding our memory of a place or experience may not be the same as another person at the same place, at the same time. However, the recollections shared are accurate to the best of the author's ability.

FIVE THIMBLES,
A Tennessee childhood memoir,
by Paula Grizzell DeMarini
ISBN-13 978-0-615-37316-4

First printing: April 12, 2011

Contributory writing by
Craig S. Brown and Rob Bowsher

Cover, book design and story
editing by Craig S. Brown

Proofreading by Katie Allen

Front cover: *Paula Grizzell, age two, going home from Oak Ridge Hospital after recovering from surgery.*

Back cover: *Grade-school pictures of the Grizzell children; from left, Elaine, Mo, Paula, Gee and John Chris*

Five Thimbles is dedicated to my late mother,
Mary Ruth Hale Grizzell,
whose faith, strength and tenacity will live on in the hearts of her children, grandchildren and great-grandchildren. She will be remembered by all who were lucky enough to cross paths with her. Her mantra: **"always rise above whatever circumstance you are in,"** glowed in everything she did, every day of her life.

Mother, I hope my love and appreciation for you bleeds through every page of this book.

Also remembering:

Santa DeMarini (1919-2004), my late father-in-law, whose zest for life was unmatched; a fearless entrepreneur.

Gail Goldsmith Yankovich (1964-2009), my strong, brave friend who, like my mother, would have done anything for her children.

Karen Blackman (1958-2009), I love you and I miss you every single day.

A special thanks

to my husband and our children for believing in me and cheering me on. Tommy, thank you for your undying love and confidence in me. To our daughter, Heidi, and her husband Matt, thank you for the idea to write a chapter about each street where I lived, as well as creative tips along the way. To our son, Chad, and his wife Katie, thank you for encouraging me to go the distance, and to baby Graham for reminding me what the pure love of a child can bring to our lives.

Without my siblings, whom I dearly love, there would be no story. Elaine...sorry about all the pee, I love you. Merle...I simply could not possibly have put these chapters together without your help. Gary...thank you for convincing me to write every day. To all three of my sisters-in-law who were kind enough to give me crucial input—Tricia DeMarini, Linda Grizzell and Lois Grizzell, thank you. I want to express my appreciation to all of my soul sisters (you know who you are) whose friendships mean the world to me and keep me grounded. I would be remiss if I did not thank my book pal, Sally Cooper of San Antonio, for urging me to move forward.

Thanks also to Rob Bowsher, a writer who gave me the jump-start I needed and convinced me I had a compelling story to tell; and to my editor and friend, Craig Brown, a graphic designer who spent countless hours working on *Five Thimbles*. Without him, this memoir of my childhood and tribute to my mother may never have been published.

Streets where I lived, in chronological order:

My family at Viking Road, 1958, about the time we put Monkeyface in the dryer and before my father lost his job. From left: me, Mother, Mo, my father holding John Chris, Elaine and Gee.

Everything I am or ever hope to be,
I owe to my angel mother.

– *ABRAHAM LINCOLN*

Preface

I TURNED EIGHTEEN in 1970, over forty years ago. From that day forward, I have had a persistent, gnawing desire to put pen to paper in hopes of describing the hardships my family endured and overcame. For over forty years, I scribbled all sorts of notes, constantly thinking the day would come when I would pull my family's story together. I have been saving dozens, if not hundreds, of my recollections in a shoebox.

Perhaps I did this because many never believed I lived in twenty-five places in my first eighteen years, or that my family never had a phone, or car, and sometimes lived without indoor plumbing or a furnace for warmth. Although I never doubted how fortunate I was to have a tremendously large, wholesome and benevolent extended family, the reason for everything that was good and right in my life was due to my courageous mother, working in tandem with those relatives.

My mother sacrificed everything for her five children, asking nothing in return. She gave us a rich quality of life nobody ever had reason to expect. She loved us deeply the instant we were born, she loved us deeply when she died at age eighty...and every minute in between.

I once read an amazing story in a periodical. As I recall, it was written as a true account and went something like this:

After a forest fire in Yellowstone National Park, forest rangers began their trek up a mountain to assess the inferno's damage. One ranger found a bird literally petrified in ashes, perched statuesquely on the ground at the base of a tree. Somewhat sickened by the eerie sight, he knocked over the bird with a stick. When he struck it, five tiny chicks scurried from under their dead mother's wings. The loving mother, keenly aware of impending disaster, had carried her offspring to the base of a tree and had gathered them under her wings, instinctively knowing that the toxic smoke would rise. She could have flown to safety but had refused to abandon her babies. When the blaze had arrived and the heat had scorched her small body, the mother had remained steadfast. Because she had been willing to sacrifice, those under the cover of her wings would live.

And so goes the story of my mother.

Five Thimbles

{ One }

MARQUETTE AVENUE

A TARNISHED AND dented thimble. It is one of my most prized possessions which belonged to my mother. I spotted it on one of our last trips to Mother's home after she passed away at age 80. There it was—sitting all alone in the center of a sixty-year-old mantle, gathering dust.

Gasping with joy, I almost lost my breath as I grabbed the thimble, clutching it against my heart. I felt as if I had discovered a million dollars. I glanced at my brothers who were wondering why I was so emotional. I was choking back the tears as I told them I found Mother's thimble; for it was this type of Mother's few possessions we treasured. It was clear from the look in my siblings' eyes that I had a valued object in my hand. I offered it to one of my brothers because I wanted him to have it as desperately as I wanted it for myself.

"Maybe we can find another thimble among Mother's things," someone suddenly said. We began searching the small, four-room "B" house and within a few short minutes we had discovered another four very old thimbles. Now, we had five thimbles. Not four thimbles. Not six thimbles. We had found five thimbles which Mother had used for years and years as she sculptured most everything we wore when we were young.

Naturally, I reasoned there was one thimble for each of her five children. The symbolism was hard to miss. When I think of the purpose of a thimble and the tasks it allows one to accomplish, my mother's strength and tenacity come to mind.

Mother's remarkable life began near McMinnville, Tennessee, on the eve of the Great Depression. Her name was Mary Ruth Hale and everyone called her Ruth. She was her father's sixth child, but she was the first of her mother's seven children. From this unique position in her family, she learned quickly to respect her elders and to nurture her juniors. She had a strong sense of family and maintained a close relationship with her parents and siblings all of her life.

She gave birth to five children. My only sister, Elaine, was born six years before me. Then my older brother, Merle, was born on my sister's second birthday. I do not know when Merle picked up his nickname, but we have called him "Mo" for as long as I can remember. Four years after Mo, I was born the middle child. Thirteen months after me, Gary was born. Mother nicknamed Gary early on, referring to him as "Gee" (pronounced with a hard "G", as in the word "glee"). We were so close in age people thought Gee and I were twins. When I was six years old, our baby brother, John Chris, came along.

We were all born in Oak Ridge, Tennessee, and lived there most of our childhood. My family was renting a small house on Marquette Avenue in Oak Ridge when I was born, January 8, 1952. Our small two-bedroom duplex had a living room and an eat-in kitchen, similar to the other houses built in our cul-de-sac. Out our front door was a small, cement slab of a porch that led to a yard almost barren of plants. There was no garage or carport, but that didn't matter as we had no car. Today, a tree stands in the front yard, planted long after we moved out.

To Mother, her children were her bundles of joy and she was proud of us almost to a fault. Somehow, she made each of us feel as if we were her favorite. She took every opportunity she could find to praise us both privately and in public, even in her final weeks on earth. During one of her cancer tests at Northside Hospital in Atlanta, the Chief Administrative Officer told her, "We're very happy to have Paula working here." "You should be," Mother proudly replied.

Mother had light brown hair and beautiful olive skin. She had a petite and pretty frame, but carried herself with the elegance of a much taller woman. Her hair turned silver at the early age of thirty-five, which infuriated her. She had a beautiful smile and loved to laugh. Mother greeted everyone with open arms, and she never met a baby or small child she didn't want to cradle in those arms. An honest opinion of Mother was that everyone who knew her held her in high esteem. My parents didn't have two nickels to rub together when they were married. Therefore, Mother did not have the means to appear prominently in society, yet her demeanor and character exalted her beyond belief.

Mother loved only one man during her life. She told us her first kiss was the one she shared with our father at the altar at age seventeen. Her purity was a cornerstone of her essence; it was as much a part of her as her right arm. Mother was stoic in ways that seemed virtually impossible. Raising our family, she nurtured one of my brothers through a life-threatening illness, and she secured my well-being after I was abducted and violated as a young teenager. With no formal training, Mother handled these incredible hardships with the skill of a professional and overcame tremendous adversity with very little resources.

Everyone has a father somewhere. It just so happened mine chose not be where his wife and five children were the majority of our lives. When I moved to Atlanta at age eighteen, I had not seen my father in several months. Earlier that year, Mother had been in Oak Ridge Hospital where she had surgery to remove cervical cancer. My father visited her in the hospital on what seemed like an ordinary day. Mother had no inclination she would never see him again. She literally did not see him again prior to her death, almost forty years later.

My father and his twin brother were the youngest of the nine Grizzell children. The twins were bright, handsome, young men. In 1927, they were the Eagle Brand Milk poster children, and were featured on a large billboard on the side of a main highway in Woodbury, Tennessee. The boys were pictured standing in a berry patch wearing matching straw hats. The caption read "The Eagle Brand Milk Boys." Frankly, they were such chubby little guys they looked as if Eagle Brand Milk was all they ingested! Being the milk poster children brought certain benefits. Not only were the twins well known, but the Eagle Brand folks kept tabs on them as they grew and photographed them often. This allowed my grandparents to have some adorable photos they normally would not have been able to afford.

My father was musically talented. He could play a number of instruments by ear. He could play piano, guitar, mandolin and violin. He could hear a tune, then sit at grandmother's old piano and play it without any training whatsoever. His fiddle was his prized possession when I was a little girl. I also remember he had a beautiful singing voice.

When I was young, my father had a steady, reliable job at the atomic energy plant in Oak Ridge. His salary was more than adequate to support our small family. But he dreamed of becoming a country-and-western musician and frequented honky-tonks where he could play his fiddle or guitar and sing competitively. He began going out at night and did not always come home at bedtime. It was not unusual for him to disappear for weeks and sometimes months at a time while I was growing up. His disappearances meant we were often unable to pay the rent, leading to a pattern of evictions and last-minutes moves. He was the reason I lived in twenty-five locations in my first eighteen years. I believe he loved his family, but he was clearly conflicted about the responsibilities of family life.

There is little else I care to say about my father. This story is not about him.

{ Two }

ROBERTSVILLE ROAD

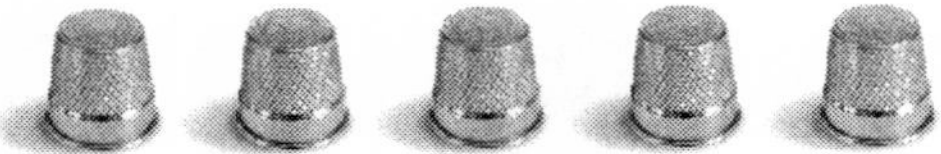

OUR FAMILY MOVED to Robertsville Road when I was a few months old. Although I have no first-hand memories of living there, the two-bedroom house is still standing. Interestingly, when Oak Ridge houses were built, they were constructed with the notion they would stand for only ten years. The houses were built hurriedly in order to accommodate the thousands of people moving to the area in the 1940s as the Manhattan Project was unfolding. General Leslie Groves, who helped supervise construction of the Pentagon, was put in charge of the Manhattan Project and selected the site where Oak Ridge was to be built.

The new houses were strategically designed in several "postage stamp" floor plans. An "A" house had a living room, eat-in kitchen and one small bedroom. A "B" house had a living room, kitchen and two bedrooms. A "C" house was L-shaped with three bedrooms. The "D" houses were huge by our standards, with four bedrooms. The "E" style was a crafty quadraplex which housed four apartments; a pair of two-bedroom apartments sandwiched between a couple of one-bedroom apartments, all under one roof. None of the models had dining rooms. The truth is the houses were built like fortresses when they were constructed and many were made of cement block. In those days, the source of heat was coal. The houses were positioned in such a way that the back doors faced the streets, making it easy for coal trucks to dump their loads of coal close to where the furnace rooms were located. Everything about it made Oak Ridge, Tennessee, a unique city like no other.

My siblings describe a hilarious event during Christmastime on Robertsville Road. Elaine was seven years old and Mo was five. They remember our father cutting our Christmas tree from the yard. Apparently, we had no tree stand, so in order to make the pine stand upright, our father nailed it to the floor in the living room! Our family always had a Christmas tree, no matter how tough things were for us financially. Even though I was too young to remember that particular season, I know from experience Mother would have sewn beautiful homemade ornaments. She crocheted dozens of little white angels which hung on our Christmas trees, secured with a loop made from yarn which doubled as an ornament hanger. Mother never required a pattern and her angels had intricate details; perfect little faces and wings stiffly starched. She also crocheted white snowflakes in all sizes for our trees. We saved the angels and snowflakes year after year, with Mother adding to the collection each season. As I recall, she gave lots of these handcrafted ornaments to special friends and family.

Mother made every Christmas holiday memorable. The kinds of things she did for us required very little money, if any. Elaine and I always received a doll for Christmas. Most years, they were handmade out of muslin with adorable, colorful faces drawn with indelible ink. One Christmas, Mother made us dolls with dark skin and braids of black yarn. Another year, we received dolls which looked Asian. Naturally, Mother used scraps of fabric to sew perfect outfits for our baby dolls. As I reflect on the times when she made ethnic dolls for us, I understand she was using them to demonstrate an important life lesson. She consistently taught her children the importance of equality.

My mother believed in the Civil Rights Movement. She often shared her views by telling us we must never consider one human being better than another. Whenever we passed the town laundromat, we would see an obvious sign stating "Whites Only." Mother never failed to explain to us how very wrong this was. It killed her that different housing in Oak Ridge was set apart depending on who you were or how well you were paid. African-Americans could only live in houses separate from others. She thought we should all be considered equal with equal opportunities and that no one person was better than the next. She insisted we treat everyone with respect. She also taught us we should expect to be treated with the same respect.

One thing is for sure: Mother was not a woman who suppressed her opinions. We always knew where she stood. Although we were well provided for while living on Robertsville Road, in later years we faced seriously tough economic times. As for Mother, fairness and living by the Golden Rule (treat others as you would like to be treated) were always a part of who she was. She may well have been thinking of her own children possibly being looked down upon someday. Even when we were living in poor conditions, Mother never allowed us to believe we lived on the wrong side of the tracks. "You can step into any room filled with the wealthiest, most educated, most attractive people in the world," she would say, "and you are no less or better than any of them."

Oak Ridge was known as "The Atomic City," "The Secret City" and "The City Behind the Gates." It has a unique history like no other city in the world. I was told Oak Ridge was chosen as the site of the atomic energy plants because the entire city could be housed in a valley. When I was a little girl, I remember hearing the adults talk about how the buildings could not easily be spotted from the air and were smothered in a thick covering of trees. I was somewhat frightened because I thought they may be referring to enemy planes flying overhead. This kind of talk always scared me, especially since we frequently received instructions on how to use the fallout shelters. By the 1950s, it was public knowledge that Oak Ridge was one of the sites which contributed to the design of the atomic bomb, and the atomic energy plants were still a target.

The plants were called X-10, Y-12 and K-25. My father worked at Y-12 and its gate was within a few miles of any of the places we lived in Oak Ridge. I remember when I was a little girl, I rode with a relative to pick up my father after work. Once inside the main gate, we passed a huge rock quarry. Between the main gate and the place where the workers were picked up, you had to pass through another guarded gate. I remember guards with firearms everywhere. Security was high and the buildings were huge in size. K-25 itself was over a mile long.

Early on, the employees did not know what they were building. My understanding was that each person had a specific task, but did not know anything about the tasks of their co-workers. Nor did the workers know what the end product was. I remember Granddaddy Hale, my mother's father, telling a story about a worker who curiously lifted a tarp which was thrown over some type of equipment. That curious worker was fired on the spot. Each person was expected to complete his designated task without asking questions. During their shift, employees were required to wear a badge called a dosimeter. These badges measured radiation exposure and they were never to leave the plant. Each employee left his or her badge in a designated spot before heading home.

When the city was being built, construction was underway twenty-four hours a day, seven days a week. Employment opportunities were abundant and hundreds of scientists and engineers were employed in Oak Ridge, as well as large numbers of ancillary workers. Many of the women who had been left behind during World War II worked at the plants. When the war was over, the women were laid off in order to provide positions for the servicemen as they returned to the states. Even though Oak Ridge did not exist on a map, the population grew to over 70,000. The average age of a resident was under 30 years. Everyone was required to wear an identification badge, including children 12 years and older, and there were gates on either end of the city which allowed guards to check for proper identification. I remember my relatives describing the billboards around town, put up as reminders for the citizens. They read:

The safety of the nation depends on you
to keep your mouth shut

What you hear here, What you see here,
What you do here, When you leave here,
Let it stay here

Those who came to Oak Ridge for the Manhattan Project were considered the best in their fields, including Albert Einstein. As I grew older, I learned many ingenious items were created under the roofs of those plants. In fact, the brilliant scientists who invented the well-known PET scanners once worked in that environment. A number of bright minds and talented people comprised the many teams of inventors. These professionals demanded the best possible teaching in the public school system. Apparently, the sentiment never changed, since *Newsweek* Magazine recently featured Oak Ridge High School on its list of top public secondary schools in the United States.

Another fun, family story comes to mind when I think of Robertsville Road. Both myself and my brother Gee were only infants and too small to remember. However, I heard Mother tell the story many times about an adventure my brother Mo went on when he was barely five years old. There was a boy in the neighborhood about the same age, who was Mo's partner in crime. My brother and his friend found some play money in one of their toy boxes. I am not sure, but I think it may have been money from a Monopoly game. Mo and the neighbor kid took the money and scurried down the road to a grocery store. You have to be familiar with Robertsville Road to know what a busy, steep and long way it was to the nearest store. The two little guys walked a distance of three miles without adult supervision.

The young boys arrived unharmed at the grocery store. The cashier immediately surmised the children had slipped away from their parents when the boys tried to buy candy bars with the play money. However, the dead giveaway that they were runaways in need of assistance was when it was noticed Mo's little muddy feet were bare! The store manager displayed much-appreciated concern when he called the Oak Ridge Police Department in order to ensure the boys made it back to their respective homes safely. Mo and his buddy were given the candy bar they so desperately sought, then they were given a free ride in the back seat of the squad car. Although they were given candy bars in exchange for the play money, what they were not given was change! This stunt was not nearly as scary as when Mother caught Mo gathering black widow spiders in a mason jar! Mo said, "See Mommy! They have red tummies!"

{ Three }

QUINCY AVENUE, 1954

A HORRIBLE ACCIDENT had occurred; I was in a coma due to a hard blow to the head. Mother's recollection of that unfortunate day was recited many times through the years, for this would be the first time the infamous Dr. Robert Bigelow entered the picture. According to my mother, Dr. Bigelow changed our lives forever.

The impact lifted me into the air. The batter had drawn the wooden baseball bat over his right shoulder, then reversed his swing with all his might, slamming me square in the back of the head as he made a full follow-through. I was just north of two years old; a mere toddler. Mo, then almost seven, was playing baseball with some of his neighborhood friends around the same age. The children were enjoying an orderly game of baseball on a beautiful, sunny afternoon. As a mischievous toddler, I had meandered into an area where I did not belong. Though it was not his fault, I understood later that the kid who struck me was mortified at the thought of hurting me.

There I lay in the grass, as limp as a rag doll. Mother, ever the level headed one, began barking orders, "You...find a phone and call an ambulance. You...bring a damp washcloth. The rest of you...stand back and be silent." She knelt beside my limp body which weighed all of thirty-five pounds, checked my airway and found that I had a steady, yet shallow pulse. I think my mother's middle name should have been "optimistic," for she was determined from the start that I was going to recover.

The emergency vehicle sped the short distance from Oak Ridge Hospital to Quincy Avenue. The technicians carefully moved my small frame onto the stretcher, supporting my tiny neck all the while. Accounts from people who witnessed the incident verified my mother's calm demeanor as I was placed in the ambulance. Mother was then escorted from the vehicle as no unauthorized personnel were allowed to ride in the cab. However, the technicians were crazy if they thought my mother was going to stay behind. Mother was not hysterical, instead she was steady, firm and all business as she convinced them she needed to ride along.

So, off we all went with the sirens screaming. Dr. Bigelow was there to greet us when we arrived at the emergency room entrance. Mother described later with great detail how he walked to the stretcher as I was lifted out of the back of the vehicle. Dr. Bigelow was a big man, with wavy grey hair and thick, black glasses. His voice was deep and he talked with a soothing tone. He knelt over me, lifted me into his arms and carried me to the triage area. After tests and X-rays were performed, the doctor told Mother there were no signs of a skull fracture. However, the swelling and inflammation due to the impact resulted in an unconscious, comatose state. Dr. Bigelow stated there was no guarantee I would ever wake up and that only time would tell.

Mother stayed in the hospital with me and never left my side. My Aunt Dixie came to our house to help with Elaine, Mo and Gee, who was only fifteen months old. Twenty-four hours passed, no new developments. Another twenty-four hours passed, nothing. A few hours later, Mother was half standing and half lying beside me in the small pediatric hospital bed when she felt my limbs begin to thrash about. I was awake alright. According to Mother, I was trying to pull the intravenous tubing out of my arm. Mother called for help from the nurses.

Unfortunately soon after, Mother was taken to a room where Dr. Bigelow could speak with her privately. During my comatose state, the doctor detected a lump on my neck the size of a hen egg. Technically speaking, there was a tumor on my thyroglossal duct. Dr. Bigelow gave the usual warning that the tumor could be malignant. I was released from the hospital with a plan for future surgery. My family was terrified.

Cancer had already struck my father's family. My Uncle John Pope Grizzell, who lived in Oak Ridge and worked at K-25, died at the early age of thirty-five. He was diagnosed with testicular cancer in the spring of 1951 and soon afterward, the cancer metastasized. He lived for six short months. I cannot say with certainty if exposure to dangerous materials at the plant contributed to his cancer. However, my mother was clearly under the impression that this was the case. My uncle's wife, Aunt Bill, was one of my mother's dearest friends. Their children, Judy and

Tim, were the closest of my sixty-two first cousins. My cousin Judy was shockingly beautiful, I really looked up to her. Tim, the only cousin with red hair, was a talented athlete who later received a football scholarship to the University of Tennessee. We loved visiting with them. When Uncle John Pope was diagnosed, he unselfishly became a patient at the Oak Ridge Nuclear Science Facility where he received radiation and a host of experimental treatments. The most prominent memory which resonated from the relatives who visited my brave uncle was his desire to be a part of finding a cure. Recently, my Aunt Laurel Grizzell shared with me that my uncle's heartfelt wish was that the small children could be spared, much like the little ones he met in the cancer ward. "I will endure anything if it means sparing these precious children," my uncle said during his treatments. These events must have played a role in Mother's fear of my impending surgery.

A few short weeks later, we returned to Oak Ridge Hospital where Dr. Bigelow removed the lump from my neck. The tumor was benign and everyone was jubilant! From what I understand, the most challenging part of the process was keeping me, a feisty two-year-old toddler, still. Dr. Bigelow had worked his magic and guided my family through this difficult time. However, in the years to come, we would turn to him again.

Our place on Quincy Avenue was awesome. It was a three-bedroom house and the exterior was painted deep red. It had a spacious yard and a shallow, swiftly-moving brook out back.

If I close my eyes, I can hear the loud noise the crickets made around the creek bed. We had wonderful neighbors, as I recall, and there were lots of children nearby. There were twin boys in the house next door named Ray and Jay. We loved to play "kick the can," "hide-and-seek" and "red rover." Sometimes, we played in the creek catching tadpoles. We did not have tricycles or bicycles of our own, so Mother kept us busy with wholesome games which did not require store-bought toys. Elaine and Mo walked to school in this safe, close-knit neighborhood.

Our family lived on Quincy Avenue for over three years, longer than any place we lived while I was growing up. In fact, we lived in most places no longer than four to eight months. Quincy was special for many reasons. One day, the postman brought Mother a letter of notification that she had won two rooms of furniture! A local furniture store had chosen her name in a drawing. A big truck delivered a red couch and chair with blonde end tables and a matching coffee table. The haul included a blonde-colored dining table and four chairs, complete with a china cabinet. A small, black-and-white television was also part of the winnings. The TV was designed to sit on a small table, and it had large, black knobs beneath the screen and a "rabbit-ear" antenna. I believe it was the only television we ever owned. I also believe it never worked properly. Coincidentally, we moved back to the very same house in 1968 for a brief time.

One huge reason this house was so special to us: it was the only one we ever owned. Ever since the city of Oak Ridge was built, all homes were owned by the government. That changed in the late 1950s and each leaser was offered an opportunity to buy his or her rental house. Purchase prices were determined by the rent paid and offered at ten times the monthly amount. The rent on our house was fifty dollars. Therefore, the purchase price on our perfect, little red-frame home, with an acre lot, next to a beautiful babbling brook, in a desirable neighborhood and with excellent schools, was five thousand dollars. Five thousand dollars!

There was a heated discussion at our house the day we became homeowners. Mother hit the roof when she learned my father sold the house the same day for a fifteen-hundred-dollar profit. I do not remember the details of the argument my parents had that day. However, I do remember what we did with the fifteen hundred dollars.

Thanks to that transaction, our family embarked on the only vacation we ever took. The six of us drove to Daytona Beach, Florida, in a borrowed car. I was almost six years old and I remember the trip well. Elaine was allowed to sit in the middle of the front bench seat. Seatbelts were unheard of. Gee and I took turns lying under the back windshield during the lengthy ride to Florida. I remember the motel where we stayed in Daytona. It was called The Seabreeze and it was a long, concrete structure located right on the beach. Somehow, we found out that Pat Boone's milkman was staying at the motel during the same time. When we heard this, we thought we were in the presence of a celebrity. To us, it was as if Pat Boone himself was staying right next door! However, there is but one prominent memory burned in my brain from what was to become a disastrous weekend.

None of us had ever seen the ocean before, not even Mother. Certainly, we were not wise to some of the more well-known hazards. As soon as our bare feet hit the sand, we ran toward the crashing waves. We played for a few short minutes when Mo, who was ten years old, began screaming bloody murder! He had spotted a Portuguese man-of-war floating in the water. Jellyfish are often camouflaged by the reflections of the sun as it dances on the colorful shades of the ocean. The cunning sea creature floated, disguised as a purple and red rubber toy. Mo reached forward and grabbed the jellyfish. Instantly, its tentacles wrapped around Mo's hands, covering his skin with poisonous stingers. Whatever time remained of the vacation was spent in the motel with Mo, who was writhing in pain. I clearly remember him lying on the orange shag carpet on his stomach with his arms outstretched, moaning. My heart broke for him. Gee and I were huddled together in the corner of the room, watching as Mother tried everything she could think of to ease his discomfort. Mother quieted us by sweetly singing. She challenged us to be still and quiet for Mo's sake. It seemed the only thing that helped him was the passage of time.

None of us went back to the ocean. That visit to Daytona was the only time I left the state of Tennessee, prior to moving to Georgia at age eighteen.

{ Four }

VIKING ROAD, 1958

JOHN CHRIS WAS born when I was six years old. In those days, women were knocked out with ether during the birth of a child. When Mother woke up, a nurse handed her the baby. Mother said, "You have made a mistake. That is not my baby! I know what my babies look like and he is not my baby!" John Chris had burning, reddish-orange hair and big, swirling curls. None of her other four kids had curls or red hair. His skin was porcelain. As a matter of fact, the one picture my mother always had in her wallet until the day she died, was one of John Chris as a little tyke with beautiful skin and red curls. The rest of us amused ourselves for hours on end playing with John Chris. He was spoiled rotten with four big brothers and sisters at his beck and call. We loved him so.

Our place on Viking Road was an "E2" apartment. This meant we rented a two-bedroom unit in a large building which housed three other apartments. All five kids slept in one of the bedrooms and the apartment had no air conditioning. Mo and Gee slept on black wrought-iron bunk beds. Whoever slept on the top bunk would often rotate the pillows outside a small window to cool them on hot summer nights. Elaine and I had a rollaway bed and John Chris' baby crib was between us and our brothers. What I remember most about that rollaway bed is not how uncomfortable it was, but how I peed on Elaine every night! Inevitably, she would wake up wet from my pee and stomp her feet. She did not fuss at me, but clearly it was an inconvenience. She was in her early teens by now, so smelling like urine was not a good thing. Although I was a bed wetter until I was about thirteen years old, Mother never once ridiculed or scolded me, nor would she allow anyone else to do so. She simply washed my sheets and hung them on the clothes line to dry, every single day without complaining. It was just part of her routine.

We never, ever owned a car, but we borrowed them from time to time. My father had a car once for a half day when we lived on Viking Road. He borrowed an old Studebaker so we could drive to McMinnville and visit our families, one hundred miles away. Gee and I were so excited when my father said that maybe he would buy the Studebaker. We almost had a car! That was, until we wrecked it. Mother was in the passenger seat with John Chris in her lap, Gee and I were in the backseat. My father was driving down a curvy, valley road with a cliff on one side. Suddenly, the brakes went out in that beat-up old car and my father had to choose between hitting the rocky mountainside or going off the cliff. Mother braced with her foot to save John Chris from going through the window on impact. She broke her ankle and foot in the crash and bruised her arm. Nobody else got a scratch, but the car was undriveable. Soon, a man came by and gave us a ride to McMinnville. My father left the Studebaker on the side of the road and we never went back for it. It was a scary ride, but later we laughed so hard about leaving that car on the side of the mountain. Hilarious!

Although we did not live on Viking Road very long, it was a happy time. I remember Mother sewing her heart out as she made me a new dress for my 6th birthday. It was two-toned in purple and pink with a fabric remnant of lavender cotton across the shoulders and a light-colored band at the bottom. Without fail, she always hand-crafted beautiful outfits for us. On this day, a few neighborhood kids came over for birthday cake. We played "Hide the Thimble," which was Mother's version of "I Spy." The object of the game was to spot Mother's hidden thimble. Whoever was "it" hid the thimble while everyone else closed their eyes. Then, we all walked around the room with instructions to declare "I Spy!" when we spotted the thimble. When we did, we sat patiently while the other children looked for it. Whoever spotted the thimble first had the privilege of hiding it next. We often played for hours.

The only cat my family ever owned was a gray and white alley cat named Monkeyface. Monkeyface lived outside as Mother forbade us from having pets in the house. Gee and I sneaked that kitty inside whenever we could. We dressed her up by tying a handkerchief on her head like a bonnet. She scooted around trying to stay clear of our grasp. The kitchen in the apartment was very small. It was furnished with a washer and dryer; one of the few places where we had that luxury. I only remember part of this story, but Mother was happy to fill in the gaps whenever someone wanted to hear what happened with me, Gee and Monkeyface.

What I recall is getting in a heap of trouble due to the hole in the screened door. According to Mother, she came into the small kitchen having heard a noisy clatter and the cat screeching loudly. I was standing next to Gee with a guilty look on my face. When questioned, I told Mother I had helped Gee get into the clothes dryer, then Gee helped me get into the clothes dryer. Afterwards, we put Monkeyface in the clothes dryer and turned it on. When we opened the dryer door, Monkeyface jumped out lightening fast. She slammed into the cabinet which was in front of the dryer, then ricocheted sideways spiraling a foot above the floor and made a hole in the screened door as she exited. We never saw Monkeyface again. I was so sad, I could not tell her I regretted putting her in the clothes dryer. I did not mean to hurt her. I got a lecture from Mother about how "every action has its consequences." Poor Monkeyface.

My brother Mo was four years older than me. He was always a really good boy, but he found unique ways of getting into mischief, as well. Mother was not pleased when an angry parent of a neighborhood boy knocked on the door one afternoon. The lady was fuming! It seems Mo and some of his buddies (we are talking about ten-year-old boys here) thought it would be cute to trick her son, who was the neighborhood bully. Her son boasted that he could get high from smelling gasoline fumes or by drinking pickle juice. Mo and the others offered him a pickle jar, so he could prove his point. One gulp is all it took before the boy threw the pickle jar exclaiming, "Hey! That's not pickle juice! That's pee!" All the boys had contributed a few ounces to the juice before offering it to the bully. Mother gave Mo a very stern lecture, while trying to conceal her smile. She could not help laughing.

At school, we always celebrated May Day with an annual circus fund raiser. All of the students participated with some sort of activity. I was in kindergarten, so my role in the circus was to jump rope. Mother made me a blue gingham outfit for the circus. She also made a crown and cape which Mo wore as May Day king for his grade. As I walked home that day with a girl who lived next door, we stopped at the Jackson Square Drug Store. I cannot explain what came over me because clearly I knew better, but I stole a small ragdoll. It was a pink and white cloth doll about the size of my hand. I don't remember even trying to hide my actions from the cashier; I was not exactly an experienced thief. I stuffed the limp doll inside the elastic waist band of my blue gingham pants. What I remember most is that my conscience was killing me. When I arrived home, I was sobbing so hard I could barely tell Mother what I had done. Mother said, "I will give you something to cry about!"

My mother pretty much had a "zero tolerance" policy and we could not get away with anything! She almost jerked my arm out of its socket as she pulled me out the door. She marched me back to the drug store with instructions to return the doll with an apology. The owner of the store gave me a stern look before giving Mother a look of approval. That walk home was one of the longest walks of my life for I knew what was going to happen next. Mother sent Gee outside to break off a limb for my switching. I never understood why Mother always asked Gee to get the switch. Perhaps she thought if she sent me, I would return with a little twig. She gave me something to cry about alright, but the worst part was the lecture to follow. I hoped my life of crime was over. I must admit it felt wonderful to confess my wrong doing, take my punishment and get the rewards of a big hug and an "I love you" from Mother. I knew she was just keeping me straight.

John Chris slept in a little bassinet in the living room during the day. My father was looking after us one afternoon when the baby was hungry and crying his heart out. So, my father went to the kitchen to heat a bottle of milk. In those days, babies drank from glass bottles. The only way to heat the milk was to put the bottle in boiling hot water, which took quite a bit more time than popping it in a microwave. John Chris was really screaming and I made the mistake of letting him suck on my finger. He seemed plenty content with that, but suffice it to say my father was furious! I never understood why my father was so mad at me that day. He flung his huge, John Wayne-sized hand around and slapped me in the face! "Paula Faye!" he said, "how could you?"

I can honestly say that is the only time my father struck me. He saved all his lashings for my brothers. The slap made an everlasting impression on me. I made a conscious decision that I would strive never to strike my children in the face. I found the humiliation to be unnecessary and demeaning.

Perhaps tensions were high. My father had worked at the atomic energy plant all of my life, but that was about to change. Everything was about to change. Our entire lives were about to be turned upside down. My father came home from work early one day in a bad mood. My siblings remember guards from the plant coming to our apartment to retrieve my father's dosimeter. This was odd for two reasons. For one, it was not customary to see a guard in uniform outside the gates of the plants. Secondly, there were strict guidelines that dosimeters were not to be taken away from the plant. There was talk of a chemical spill, however I do not have all the facts. My father later claimed he was near a hose which broke, spraying him with plutonium. He said someone helped him pull his worksuit off and washed him down. He also later claimed that some of the dosimeters assigned to the workers were not functioning properly and that the badges were missing the film necessary to monitor the radiation exposure.

Whatever the story was, my father was no longer employed by the Federal Government; he had lost his job. Since so much of Oak Ridge was run by the government, those unassociated with the plants were discouraged from living there. Soon, we were evicted from our apartment and we left town. We headed west in the direction of Nashville, perhaps so my father could pursue his dream of making it big in the music business.

As for Mother, she handled everything that life thrust upon her with grace. Anyone who knew Mother will tell you she hardly ever complained. Instead, she simply strived to "rise above" whatever circumstance we found ourselves in. Mother was a devout Christian and she instilled in all of us how our God is a loving and caring God, always looking over us. I remember her reciting the same bedtime prayer each night with us for many years:

Now, I lay me down to sleep
I pray thee Lord, my soul to keep
If I should die before I wake
I pray thee Lord, my soul to take
AMEN

Then, I watched as she lowered herself to her knees to pray silently...every single night.

My mother, Mary Ruth Hale, is the baby in this picture. She sits on the lap of my Great-Grandmother Collins. My Hale grandparents are standing in the back. The other children are Granddaddy's eldest, from left, Willette, Inez and Ed.

Mother, right, and her younger brother, John Leroy. They were big sibling rivals, but they were also very protective of each other.

Mother, left, with her mother and siblings. Next to Mother from left, Jane Ann, Mommy Hale holding June and John Leroy.

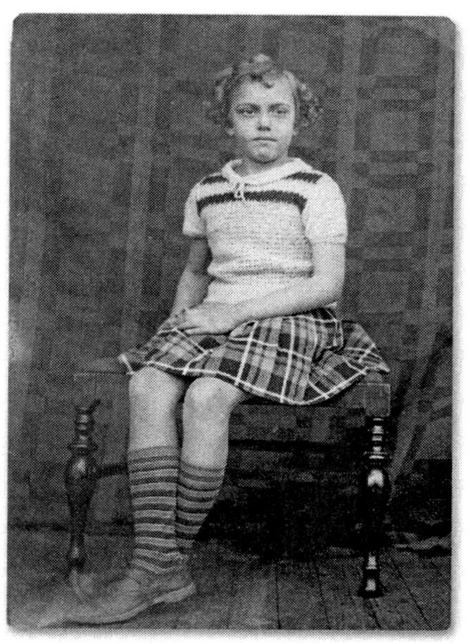

Mother as a young girl in McMinnville.

Mother, left, with a few of her Hale nieces and nephews.

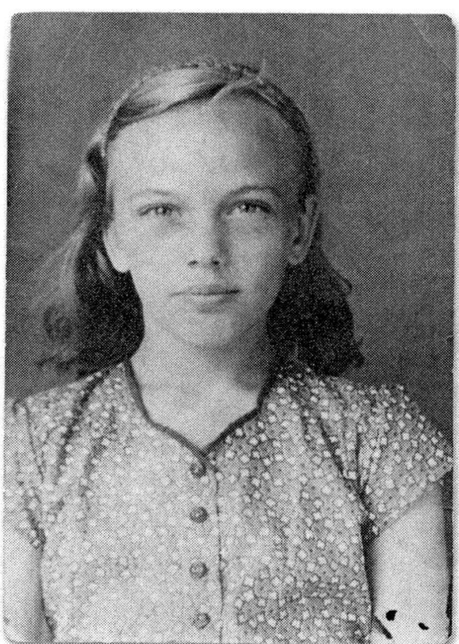

Mother at age 12.

My father, right, at age nine months, with his twin brother. This is one of many photos taken of the boys when they were the Eagle Brand Milk poster children.

My father's family at the Grizzell Farm. Granddad and Grandmother Grizzell are seated in the center, the twins are in front.

The six Grizzell brothers at the Grizzell Farm. My father and his twin, Lloyd, are in back. In front are, from left, Isaac John, Norman, John Pope and Harold.

One of many billboards erected in Oak Ridge during World War II, reminding citizens of the secret nature of the work performed.
Photo: © James E. Westcott and used with permission

My parents and my sister, Elaine. This photo shows how young my parents were when they married.

My sister Elaine, age 3, and my brother Mo, age 1.

At Aunt Faye's house, Mother is holding my brother Gee, my father is holding me and Mo is in front.

Me at five months.

Robertsville Road: Mother, me and Gee.

Two pictures of me at Oak Ridge Hospital during my recovery after surgery. Top, Mother and me on the hospital steps. Below, going home.

From left, my father, Elaine, me, Gee, Mo and Mother at my Grizzell Grandparent's 50th wedding anniversary.

Cousin Hoyt, Uncle Tim, me and cousin Susan standing by Granddaddy Hale's car.

Grade school pictures in Oak Ridge. Clockwise from top left, Elaine, Mo, Gee and me. Gee is wearing a shirt that Mother made from a fabric remnant.

Quincy Avenue: Mother wearing a dress she made.

Quincy Avenue: Mother, Gee, Mo, Elaine and me, just before my father bought and sold this house on the same day.

Quincy Avenue: Me and Gee with Oak Ridge in the background.

From left, Uncle Tim, me, Aunt June and Gee on the front lawn at my Hale grandparent's place, West End Avenue.

Photo booth snapshots. The left row is of Aunt June, my mother's sister, the middle rows are of Mother and at right is Elaine.

Me on Aunt Faye's porch with her monkey.

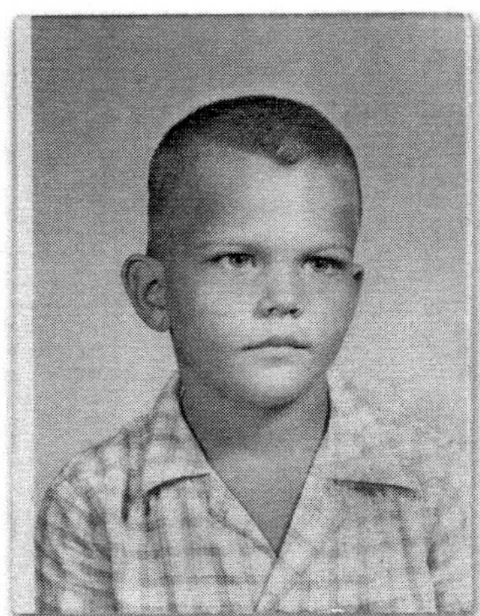

Grade school pictures of me and Gee.

Me, with cousins Penny and Nancy, wearing Grandmother Grizzell's shoes.

Viking Road: me holding John Chris.

Mother carried this picture of John Chris and herself in her wallet all of her life.

Gee with buckets of blackberries. We'd pick and sell blackberries so we could buy milk and bread.

Mother with my father's infamous fiddle.

Chamberlain Drive: me with Aunt Faye's monkey and bride doll.

Me with Aunt Faye and Uncle Clark.

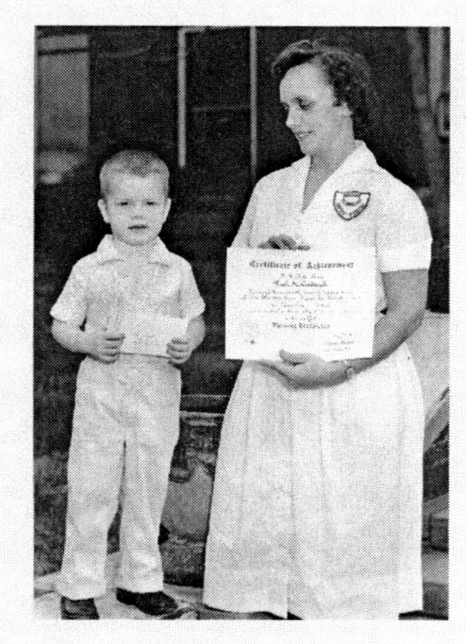

Mother and John Chris in Nashville. My mother brought my brother so often to nursing school, the school gave them both certificates.

{ Five }

CHARLOTTE AVENUE

NASHVILLE FELT LIKE the other side of the world from Oak Ridge. We rode in Granddad Grizzell's old truck for what seemed like a lifetime. The afternoon was hot and sultry when we arrived at a run-down rental house on Charlotte Avenue, in an old section of the city. The house was a big, drafty, century-old mansion that had been magnificent in its day. I figure we must have lived there for at least six months, because the bitter-cold winter has left the clearest of memories.

Every time we moved to a new place, we borrowed Granddad Grizzell's old, black Chevrolet pickup truck. We never had more than one truck load when we moved. I would not realize until years later that when we had to flee in a hurry, we left most of our belongings behind. Sometimes, my siblings and I were embarrassed to ride on the bed of that old truck. John Chris was small, so he needed to be in the front cab with Mother. The truck had a hole in the floorboard where the clutch popped as Granddad moved the gearshift. I remember so well how the road was visible through that hole beneath the clutch.

Down the rickety, narrow staircase came a parachute

which was discovered in the attic the day we moved in. My brothers had been exploring and discovered the parachute among a variety of old war relics. The slightly used, orange and white silk parachute served a multitude of purposes. Mother turned it into drapes for several windows, leaving plenty of fabric for the carefully stitched shirts she made for my brothers out of the white portion. Each had perfectly hand-sewn button holes to slip over the matching white buttons. From the orange silk, she crafted matching orange full skirts with large bows for Elaine and I. She never required patterns, but instead created unique masterpieces with every garment she made by hand. I barely recall my mother without a thimble on her finger or a crochet needle in her hand. What a pair, Mother and her thimble. Rock solid. Sturdy and strong. Forever pressing forward.

That huge house had three stories. Most likely, the rent was relatively cheap since the structure was scheduled to be demolished. In its day, the house must have belonged to a well-to-do family. It was spacious with hardwood flooring, high ceilings and crown molding that even an unsophisticated child could not miss. I remember the door knobs were lead crystal, strategically placed above huge key holes, which might have been home to antique skeleton keys. The basement had a damp dirt floor. It was dark and downright spooky. There was only one door from the basement into the house. This door opened into the bathroom constructed in the main hallway of the first floor and was blocked by an old claw-footed bathtub. The one bathroom was obviously added years after the house was designed since it consumed what had been the hallway. Every time I went into the bathroom, I had to "check out" three doors, one to the basement and one at each end of the bathroom which used to be the hallway. We had no way of knowing then how lucky we were to even have a bathroom. Over the years, some of the places where we lived had no indoor plumbing at all.

The kitchen was furnished with a metal breakfast table and a matching free-standing cabinet. It was the norm for us to be poking around looking for something to snack on. Snacks were scarce, to say the least. Gee decided to climb up to the top shelf of the cabinet. I watched as the cabinet tumbled down with Gee clinging to the very top shelf. He was hanging on for dear life as he was flung to the floor. There he lay with the shelf on top of him, and he was covered in mustard! The only food item in that cupboard was a jar of mustard, which broke and spilled over his face and neck. I was worried that Gee was badly hurt. Mother patched him up as she assessed the damages; lots of little cuts which did not require sutures. That same day, Elaine came home from school crying. She had started a new school and the only shoes she had to wear were Mother's house slippers. She was embarrassed, as anyone would be.

Each room housed an enormous fireplace inlaid with marble, clothed with meticulously carved mantles. The fireplaces were the only form of heat and were large enough for a grown man to walk into, standing upright. One frigid winter night, all seven of us were huddled together in the main room trying to keep from freezing. The small stack of firewood had dwindled down to nothing. I remember John Chris' toes were stiff and dark, as if they were frostbitten. The broad doorways in the living room were draped with sections of the parachute. Mother had stretched perfectly fitting portions of the tightly woven silk across the doors and windows, in order to trap the warm air into the room. The only furniture I remember in this house was our rollaway bed and a few wooden chairs. Therefore, there was practically no furniture in this room.

I remember this night because it was my 7th birthday. On this date every year, I was a celebrity. I felt famous to have the same birthday as Elvis Presley, January 8th. Mother managed to light one candle to stand in the homemade fudge we pretended was my birthday cake. Her special homemade fudge tasted much better than any cake could ever taste. Elaine, Mo, Gee and Mother were singing *Happy Birthday* to me as my father was glancing all around the room. My father was not usually around, but on this day he was present bigger than life. He had been searching for anything to burn in the fireplace. All eyes were on him as he looked up, down and all over the place. Then, his eyes fixated on Mo. My brother was sitting in the only wooden chair which remained. As the room became silent, my father paused and said to Mo, "Get up son!" My father grabbed the chair out from under Mo, broke it into pieces and pitched it into the sparsely burning embers.

When my father tossed the chair into the fireplace, he moved with a great amount of strength and deliberation. Soon, the flames were several feet high, but not for very long since the chair burned so quickly. I will never forget the look on Gee's face when my father tossed that chair into the fireplace. All of us were getting more and more upset since what little furniture we had would soon be gone. We were mortified!

Often times the power company turned our electricity off due to non-payment, in which case Mother improvised by pretending we were "camping out," making adventures out of undesirable situations. When my father burned the chair, there was no way to shield us from that shocking act. Honestly, we laughed about it many times in years to come. When my siblings are together, one of us usually says to Mo, "Get up son!" Because of Mother's amazing attitude, we learned laughter played a big role in "rising above" and moving ahead, as if everything was normal.

The neighborhood on Charlotte Avenue was being torn down, bit by bit, and our house was surrounded by the sterile feeling of concrete. The side yard had no grass at all. Instead, it was the parking lot of a Dairy Queen. The only thing that stood between us and an endless supply of chocolate-dipped ice cream cones and banana splits was a gravel parking lot…and money.

Every evening at closing time, Mother gathered us together in the dark room whose window overlooked the DQ. A kind, old, black gentleman, who managed the store, took advantage of this time each night to practice his tap dancing. We loved to watch him as he danced his heart out on the sidewalk under the neon lights. He tapped and tapped, sporting a makeshift top hat. I was convinced he was the smiley, old man I had seen tap dancing with Shirley Temple as she sang *The Good Ship Lollipop*. It had to be him! I must have had an amazing fantasy imagination, because I was easily convinced that my grand notions were true; like those about the DQ manager.

Gee and I thought for sure we had hit the jackpot when Mo got a job at Dairy Queen, picking up and burning the trash. Mo, who was about ten years old, was paid only in ice cream. Sometimes, he would treat the younger children to an ice cream cone or a chocolate milkshake when he got off work. I seem to remember the manager also allowed him to bring food home, which would ordinarily have been discarded. I was sure we were the only reason he took the job. (Yes, of course, Mo worked at Dairy Queen so he could bring leftovers home.)

The funniest sight I ever saw happened when Aunt Inez and Uncle Fred came to visit one day. Aunt Inez was my mother's sister and they brought their five children to play in the old mansion. That put ten of the sixty-three first cousins in the house at one time. We "ripped and tore," as Mother called it. Uncle Fred gave the boys a handful of money instructing them to bring back ice cream from next door.

The ice cream, however, was not the best part. The best part was witnessing my Cousin Leslie's pet monkey gripping her very own cone of ice cream. Their family owned a number of monkeys through the years, which apparently made interesting house pets. This monkey was named Judy. She was a Capuchin breed, which is easily recognized as an "organ grinder's monkey." She was truly a smart, exotic pet. She could perform simple tasks, such as peel oranges or crack open walnuts. Judy was extremely attached and loyal to Uncle Fred and his family. Judy had been a part of that family since she was an infant. She blew kisses on command and often smacked her lips as she swayed back and forth, hugging herself with her long arms. As I recall, she loved to admire herself in the mirror. Judy seemed to groom herself by straightening her fancy red vest, which was trimmed with gold rick-rack. She would also lick her fingers so she could moisten wild hairs on her head to slick them down. She had a dark gray body with a white face, throat and chest. The top of her head was jet black, as if she were wearing a cap.

The hilarious climax of the evening was when the room fell dead silent as Mother asked Uncle Fred, "Why are there tears running down that monkey's face?" I nearly fell out of my seat when I heard him explain the monkey was crying because it had measles! A monkey with measles? You had to know my mother to understand how opposed she was to having animals in the house. We often gave her a hard time because she would not allow us to have a dog. Honestly, she probably thought it would be one more mouth to feed. Seeing Judy made me think of our cat, Monkeyface. I was missing that old alley cat and wondered where she was.

My father was often away from home for brief periods of time, however when we moved to Nashville this became a nasty habit. He was gone for weeks in a row and what money he did earn did not find its way home to his wife and children. I always believed he intended to support us, but luck did not seem to follow him. Occasionally, he wrote checks which were returned for insufficient funds. The debt collectors hounded Mother in his absence. This was when Mother really had to start scraping to make ends meet. She never said one negative word about our father during that time.

As I recall, failure to pay the rent for more than 90 days was sure to get the eviction process started. I hated when the notices started arriving. Mo got really good at determining who was knocking at the door to serve warning. Thirty days... fifteen days...three days until we had to vacate. Where would we go this time? Would Mother manage to keep us together for a while longer? I could see the pain in her eyes, staring back at the messenger. We were just people with no names to him, but we were Mother's very heart and soul. Five naïve children making each day count to the fullest.

She kept our minds on happy thoughts by storytelling, singing, reading…anything she could think of to make the hours together enjoyable. Thinking back on the tough times, I do not ever remember feeling sad. The credit for that goes to my mother. She could have authored *The Power of Positive Thinking* or *You Cannot Afford The Luxury of a Negative Thought,* if she had had the means. Optimism was the demeanor she wore. The older I get, the more I realize it was sheer courage and faith.

My mother provided for us with more jobs than I can name. Her first job was in a blackberry factory where she sorted out bad berries on a conveyor belt. She babysat for friends in exchange for garden vegetables and fruits. She cooked and cleaned professionally, all the while caring for her own children.

She was a master at crocheting, making baby booties and caps on assignment. We often remarked she could probably crochet a house! She decided to become a nursing assistant and she often brought John Chris with her to class. At her graduation, the school presented her with two certificates: one was her license to be a nursing assistant and the other was an honorary diploma for John Chris.

We walked everywhere since we had no automobile. We did not really need a car since the only places we went were church, school and the store. I don't know how we managed to make it through school. Mother was so busy with all of her jobs, she could not possibly help us with homework. We seldom completed a school year in the same school and we never had essentials, like notebook paper. I remember borrowing notebook paper from classmates every single day.

There was never a question on Sunday mornings as to whether we would attend church services. Mother made that decision long before any of her children were born. Our church, Charlotte Avenue Church of Christ, was just a few blocks away. The building was gigantic and ornate, and was a Nashville landmark until it was torn down recently. I remember the distinct smell of its rich, dark wood on the beautiful walls and ceiling. I especially loved the balcony where Gee and I always sat. It was in that antique building one day that I was baptized for the remission of my sins by Batsell Barrett Baxter, who was preaching in a gospel meeting.

Years later, when I was fourteen, my Aunt Jane Ann took Gee and I to see the movie, *The Sound Of Music*. As I watched Julie Andrews make the von Trapp children matching play clothes from pairs of draperies, I believed in my heart Julie Andrews had stolen Mother's idea. I remember the five of us walking to church on Charlotte Avenue in our orange and white parachute outfits, so perfectly tailored by Mother. It was at that moment I realized she was truly a marvelous seamstress.

Although Mother was an artisan with needle and thread, her finest pattern was the one she created day by day as she guided and protected her five children in uncertain times. To borrow from Charles Dickens, "it was the best of times, it was the worst of times" living in that old house. Thanks to my mother, most of my thoughts gravitate to positive memories when I think of Charlotte Avenue.

{ Six }

SETTLE COURT

WHAT DID IT mean? Mother was frightened we would be taken from her if she could not properly provide for us. People were questioning the number of days Gee and I missed school. They were asking why we sometimes came to school hungry. They were making home visits unannounced. Somehow that summer, we made our way to a government-subsidized apartment complex in Nashville on Settle Court. It was then the decision was made for me to spend the upcoming school year at Aunt Faye's house, about forty miles away in Murfreesboro. I was crazy about my Aunt Faye and completely in favor of the decision.

I remember Settle Court well enough, although I was not there much of the time. I recall a bare, two-bedroom apartment with white linoleum flooring. Whatever furniture we didn't burn at Charlotte Avenue was left behind anyway as we fled in a hurry. The bulk of the time I spent at Settle Court was during Christmas vacation from school. I was so happy to see Mother, Elaine and my brothers. I cannot remember my father being there. Mother made fudge early on Christmas Eve, then took a short nap before going to work. Late in the evening, Mo walked Mother to the bus stop so she could catch a ride to Baptist Hospital, where she had started working the night shift as a nursing assistant. Mo, all of eleven years old, was worried for her safety since it was late and dark, and we lived in a bad part of town. Then he hurried back to the apartment so he and Elaine could watch over us.

We had a rickety Christmas tree covered with Mother's crocheted angels and icicles. It was the best tree I ever saw because I was with my siblings! We would not have had Christmas presents if it weren't for the big truck full of toys which canvassed the project neighborhood. Looking back, I am certain some charity sponsored Christmas for all the children in the projects. The truck carried dozens of dolls for the neighborhood girls. All dolls were alike; they were tall, dressy dolls whose joints were not flexible. The boys were given plastic baseballs attached to plastic baseball gloves. The toys were splendid, but being together was what made Christmas special.

When I went to Settle Court for the holidays, I was dressed in the finest garments I had ever had. Aunt Faye had dressed me head to toe, new blue shoes and all. Although proud of my new things, I felt bad because I had a warm coat and the others did not. I was heartsick. My siblings were gathered around me, firing questions about my new school and what it was like in Murfreesboro. The most wonderful part of Christmas vacation that year was helping Mother with her strenuous schedule. When the kids were in school during the day, she had to take care of John Chris and then she worked the night shift at the hospital. She must have been so tired, but she never complained. I don't think living on Settle Court was a happy time.

{ Seven }

CHAMBERLAIN DRIVE

I WAS NAMED after two people, my maternal grandmother Pauline Cooley Hale, and my father's dear sister Edith Faye Grizzell Bowling. It's hard to imagine life without any of my wonderful aunts and uncles, but I know I wouldn't be the person I am today without Aunt Faye's guidance, love and support.

I thought Aunt Faye, my father's sister, had first come into my life when I went to live with her during second grade. My father's refusals to pay rent and the ensuing evictions led us to believe the state of Tennessee might split up our family. To prevent this terrible situation, my mother accepted Aunt Faye's offer to take me into her home. I would learn later that Aunt Faye slipped money regularly to my mother and did whatever she could to help raise my siblings and I. She had actually been involved in our upbringings all of our lives.

Aunt Faye married a gentleman who managed the VA hospital's dietary department. Uncle Clark was a kind man with a great sense of humor. Clearly, he was loyal and dedicated to his family, proven each day as he never failed to provide for them. He was well-respected in the community. "Come over here, I'm going to box your ears," he would say to tease my brother Gee, who would have been six at the time. Uncle Clark always made us laugh and feel welcome.

I was enthusiastic about spending the second-grade school year with Aunt Faye and her family. Their two-story home was located in Murfreesboro, Tennessee, about an hour drive from Nashville. It had three bedrooms downstairs and one bedroom upstairs, and it had the loveliest gardens I'd ever seen. Aunt Faye always brought fresh flowers into the house and over to her neighbors. She was a master gardener who loved sharing her prize roses, mums and gladiolas with family and friends. In fact, the colorful blooming plants overtook the grass, leaving a narrow straight stretch of sidewalk as the only place to step in the front yard.

Aunt Faye worked as a registered nurse at the VA hospital. I loved the look and smell of her uniform. Her white starched cap, navy cape, and white stockings made her even more regal than she already was. She wore classic clinic nursing shoes, polished to perfection each night by Uncle Clark. No matter how sick you were, Aunt Faye could make you feel better with her presence alone. Her bedside manner was as healing as it was effortless.

Aunt Faye and Uncle Clark had two daughters who were teenagers when I came to live with them. The younger daughter, Shirley, had an outgoing personality and worked hard to welcome me. Every morning, the girls woke up early to perform their chores, including gardening duties, which they taught me how to do as well. When they learned I was a bed wetter, they awakened even earlier, at 4:30 a.m., to take me to the bathroom. If I had already wet the sheets, Shirley would say something like, "Groovy! Now we will not have to go to the bathroom, let's sleep another hour." They also helped me maintain the elaborate rubber sheet that was placed on the bed to protect the mattress from my accidents. In Aunt Faye's house, like in my other aunt's and uncle's homes, everyone served one another.

What I also loved about living there was the formal but comfortable atmosphere. I was always called Paula Faye in the house. Aunt Faye sometimes allowed us to drink Coca-Cola on the porch when we were snapping peas or shucking corn. My mother never allowed us to drink what she called "that old black burning juice," so it was a treat to have it as often as we did in Aunt Faye's house. Meals were served on a regular schedule, in the dining room, in precise portions and always on clean plates with fine silver and crystal.

The family meals were all cooked by Henrietta, Aunt Faye's housekeeper for over 40 years. Some of my fondest childhood memories are the times I spent with Henrietta in the kitchen. She would tell me all kinds of stories, and animate them with her deep, belly laughs. Her big freckles and dimples also helped make her one of the friendliest and most approachable people I've ever known. While we talked, she loved to sit me up on her steel stool which doubled as a stepladder, so I could dry the plastic melamine dishes after she washed them so thoroughly. When Aunt Faye wasn't looking, Henrietta would sneak cookies, homemade desserts, extra bacon strips and other treats to me. She also gave Shirley her very first cigarette. I think it was a Pall Mall. Henrietta never ate at the dining room table with the family, even when Aunt Faye and Uncle Clark invited her to do so. She always pulled her stool up to the kitchen counter and ate her meals there. Whether it was a line society drew, or one she drew herself, Henrietta never crossed the line between wealthy people and their domestic help.

Henrietta lived with her husband in a house located about 30 minutes from Aunt Faye's house. Every night, Uncle Clark drove her home while Shirley and her sister cleaned the dinner dishes. Henrietta never had offspring of her own, but as she demonstrated so often with me, she enjoyed being around children immensely. She dearly loved Aunt Faye's daughters.

We walked everywhere from Aunt Faye's house. School was a safe and short walk and on Sundays, we all strolled to church. Uncle Clark believed families should always walk together. Aunt Faye bought me a beautiful outfit for church and other special occasions; the skirt and the matching blue shoes made me feel like a princess. Aunt Faye also gave me a Bible and I never left home on Sundays without it.

Aunt Faye and Uncle Clark owned two cars, but Aunt Faye never learned how to drive. (As I recall, Shirley snuck the car out occasionally before obtaining a driver's license, but never got caught.) Most of the time, Uncle Clark drove their 1958 Pontiac. It had a white body, green roof, a wide green stripe down the side, big fenders and an Indian head hood ornament. He never left home without one of his English twill driving hats, which were his trademark, so to speak. It was fun to ride in that car on Saturdays to Pope Taylor's Barbecue Joint on the edge of town where the food was smoked onsite.

One of Aunt Faye's favorite drives was to the Grizzell Farm in McMinnville. Sometimes, Aunt Faye would bring Henrietta along to give Grandmother Grizzell a day off from cleaning. Throughout the drive, Uncle Clark would smoke one cigar after another. In fact, Uncle Clark smoked habitually in and out of the house. His feet always hurt him, so when he was home we often found him smoking cigars in his favorite recliner. Aunt Faye hated those cigars and the stench they left behind, but that never stopped Uncle Clark from lighting up each and every day.

Aunt Faye loved to take us girls to cultural venues. We went to museums, art shows, and zillions of antique markets. Antique markets were her favorites. Uncle Clark could never understand why Aunt Faye always felt compelled to buy something at those markets. Maybe, it was payback for all those cigars. Cuckoo clocks were another one of Aunt Faye's passions. There were several in the house, ticking and going off 24/7. The squeaking from the hardwood floors was about the only sound that could drown out those clocks. Aunt Faye also collected stamps and plates from all over the world. In particular, I loved the plates with Scarlet O'Hara and Rhett Butler. She had a plate for each of the Presidents of the United States.

A symbol of wealth in 1950s Tennessee was a piano. Aunt Faye and Uncle Clark had an impressive one, but it was the two keepsakes on the piano that we all remember more. The first was Aunt Faye's bride doll, which was as tall as I was. No one was allowed to touch the doll. The other keepsake was a stuffed monkey that stood on its feet. It just begged to be a children's toy, but like the doll, no one was allowed to play with the monkey. (Sometimes, when Aunt Faye was at work, Shirley let me hold the monkey.)

It is interesting how certain things remain a vivid memory. In Aunt Faye's bathroom, there was a toothbrush holder attached to the wall. It had teeny doors for individual toothbrushes. Each door was engraved with the family members' names…my toothbrush laid across the top. For fun, we entertained ourselves with the heat register, a huge grate that encompassed the hallway floor. It could blow our dresses up over our heads and made us girls feel like Marilyn Monroe. We could stand on it to keep warm when we were wearing shoes. When we were barefoot, we had to jump over the register or risk having our soles scorched in mere seconds.

Holidays at Chamberlain Drive were always a treat. Henrietta would cook up a storm of desserts and other food items which went well with Coca-Cola. Aunt Faye would always serve her guests fresh orange juice in her special juice glasses. Aunt Faye was a wonderful hostess and a prolific note writer. Every day, she wrote five to six notes. It was her favorite way to extend kindness to her family, friends and neighbors. I'm forever grateful to her for teaching me how to write notes for every occasion.

I'll also be indebted to her for the way she handled my homesickness. Even though Aunt Faye and her entire family treated me like I was one of their own, I missed my mother and siblings terribly. Aunt Faye and Shirley would take turns holding me whenever my homesickness was too much for me to handle. I would cry for hours and the pain felt like my sternum was breaking in half.

One day, my school class was taking a field trip to Nashville to see a replica of the Parthenon. Aunt Faye thought it would be the perfect opportunity for me to reconnect with my family. Before I left, she gave me a dime and the phone number of my family's next-door neighbor, since my family had no phone. To this day, I can remember all the lush trees and beautiful flowers that surrounded the Parthenon and the aroma of freshly cut grass that pervaded the air. It's an enormous place in the middle of Nashville's Centennial Park. My attention shifted though when I spotted a phone booth in the park. I snuck away from the class, but at seven years old I wasn't tall enough yet to reach a pay-phone receiver. I tried so hard to reach the coin drop and receiver. All my futile jumping and reaching eventually caught my teacher's attention. She didn't have the time or the patience to understand what I was doing. No doubt I would have been in trouble if the teacher knew I never made it inside the Parthenon. She simply ordered me to get back on the bus with the other children as we were leaving.

As the bus pulled out of Nashville, I could see the

government housing project where my family was residing. The huge brick building had one door and one window per family. Seeing children playing in the yard there made me heartsick. My brothers and sister were within yelling distance, but I couldn't reach them. I was on a bus heading back to my school, over forty miles away. I recall putting my head in my wadded-up sweater so the children would think I was sleeping, but I cried so hard it was difficult to take a deep breath. My teacher did not know what was wrong, but she sat close by and attempted to console me. She gave me her apple.

To make matters worse, on my walk home from school that day I found another phone booth. I lagged behind Shirley a few feet so I could sneak into the booth. This phone booth had a built in seat. I thought for sure I would reach my family this time. With Aunt Faye's dime, I stood on the seat trying over and over to call the number I held in my little hand. After what seemed to be a hundred attempts, I gave up and headed back to Aunt Faye's house. I was too young to know that a dime wasn't enough money for a long-distance call from Murfreesboro to Nashville. My heart was broken when I had to tell Uncle Clark I never went inside the amazing venue. As always, he turned it into an adventure gone haywire, helping me laugh it off.

Shirley was wonderful to me, especially when she realized how homesick I was. The girls had the entire upstairs of the house to themselves, "our suite" as they used to call it. As anyone can imagine, having that much space was a big deal for teenage girls. They were just barely old enough to begin dating. You'd think that adding a seven-year-old into that environment would cramp their style, but they always made me feel like I belonged there. They never treated me as if I were in their way. I may have been young and naïve, but I was keenly aware that Shirley hated Uncle Clark's insistence that her date come into the house for a long chat before taking her out to eat or to a movie. Yep, the boys had to pass the Uncle Clark test.

However, Uncle Clark did have the wool pulled over his eyes occasionally by Shirley. Once she had some girlfriends over to spend the night. We all went upstairs to go to bed and we did not see Uncle Clark or Aunt Faye again until the next morning. If they had come up to say good night, they would have walked in on Shirley and her girlfriends playing "strip poker"! Undoubtedly, Shirley thought I was sound asleep, but I heard and saw everything. The girls had a deck of cards and the loser of each hand had to take off an article of clothing. The hilarious part was each girl started the game with several layers of shirts, skirts, scarves, you name it. They played until some unfortunate person ended up in her bra and underpants. The giggling going on in that upstairs suite was loud enough to wake the dead, but it never woke Uncle Clark. He thought his girls were perfect.

The sisters had matching dressers in their bedroom, filled with make-up and special keepsakes. Shirley made sure my hair ribbons were tied properly every single day, and she would always tie my dress sashes in perfect bows. With her sister's help, she braided my hair. They would braid my hair so tight my eyes would slant, but just a few moments later, my hair would loosen up so I could wear my matching ribbons. Shirley never let me leave the house without matching ribbons. The girls were terrific teenagers who later became upstanding educated citizens. Shirley worked as a registered nurse with advanced education at St. Jude's Children's Hospital in Memphis. She was intimately involved with very specialized work in cancer treatments.

Like Shirley, and like Aunt Faye, I too wanted to become a nurse. But first, I had to leave Tennessee. When I was 18, I told Aunt Faye I wanted to move to Atlanta. She knew how difficult this decision was for me because it would mean I'd have to leave my family. She also knew it was the best time for me to make this move. After giving me all the reassurance anyone could ever ask for, Aunt Faye loaned me $100 for this journey. I don't often think of people in terms of their money, but I will never forget the dime Aunt Faye gave me for the Parthenon trip and the $100 she bequeathed for my one-way trip to Atlanta.

My bus ticket cost $12. For only the second time in my life, I left the state of Tennessee, heading for the big city. I enrolled in a four-month government program to become a medical assistant. The program arranged housing for all us young women. My residence was in the garage apartment of a wealthy family near Chastain Park, in Atlanta, that had four young children. I took care of the children at night and on weekends in exchange for room-and-board and an additional $11 per week. After cashing my first paycheck, I put a ten-dollar bill in an envelope and mailed it to Aunt Faye. Instead of accepting this first installment on my loan repayment, she mailed the money back to me and forgave the debt. Her generosity knew no bounds. And she wrote to me every single week.

As soon as I completed the program, I found a job in downtown Atlanta with a private medical practice. I also moved into a one-bedroom apartment with eleven other girls. To pay the rent, I worked four additional jobs: sales clerk at a toy store in "Underground Atlanta" on Sunday afternoons, sales clerk in Sears and Roebuck's womens' clothing department on Tuesday and Thursday evenings, babysitter on Saturdays and "medical sitter" on Friday nights at Emory University Hospital. My biggest break was a job offer which allowed me to teach in Atlanta at Bryman's School of Medical Assistants for $5.00 per hour. Every month, I mailed $20 to my siblings, a commitment I had made to them before I left Tennessee. Less than a year later, I began taking night classes at a community college. Eventually, I enrolled in nursing school. A busy oncologist recruited me a few months prior to my graduation to become a chemotherapist, a position I would hold for 16 years.

Aunt Faye visited me twice while I lived in Atlanta prior to my nineteenth birthday. On her first trip, she brought me a can of mace and a device that sounded like a siren. She was always looking out for my safety and well-being. We were walking on Peachtree Street just under the famous population sign when my aunt demonstrated how to spray the mace. She accidentally walked into the mist and it blinded her for a moment as she fell to the sidewalk. We actually had a great laugh over the incident.

I'll never forget the time when we went to see the movie, *The Last Picture Show*. The bus ride cost us 35 cents each. The movie ticket was more expensive, but we didn't stay for the whole show. As soon as Cybill Shepherd bared her breasts on screen, Aunt Faye hurried us out of the theater. She wasn't going to stand for "that indecent act." She informed me that Uncle Clark had been working at a movie theatre in Murfreesboro since his retirement and that she would see the movie there later by herself!

The last time I saw Aunt Faye was in 2004. Her health had deteriorated to the point that she needed to live in an assisted-living facility. When I walked in that day, she glanced at me and said, "Paula Faye! You look like me!" But that's not my lasting memory of this incredible woman. I'll always remember her as the kind-hearted person who wrote notes every day, the hard-working nurse with the healing touch and the generous aunt who helped out my family financially and in so many other ways. I'm honored to be named after her and blessed to have had her as my guardian angel for so many years.

{ Eight }

GOLDEN FARM

THE SUMMER AFTER I lived with my Aunt Faye, my siblings and I were scattered about for a couple of months as my family searched for a new place to live. Elaine stayed with our Hale grandparents, Mo and Gee were with Aunt Dorothy on her dairy farm and I lived with my Aunt Jane.

My father's sister, Aunt Jane, was a beautiful, mild-mannered woman who found good in everything. She and her husband, Uncle Ward, ran a traditional family farm a few miles outside of McMinnville, Tennessee. Their last name was Golden and on their large farm they raised sheep, cows and horses, and they had numerous fruit orchards. I especially remember the honey-bee hives that my Uncle Ward had below the barn in the main pasture. He sold the honey in jars that had a picture of a bee on the label, and he stored the honey in a storm cellar beneath his garage. The first time I ever saw sheep being sheared was on this farm. There was nothing at all inhumane about the process, but I hated to see the sheep strapped down for shearing. It was only a haircut, I rationalized, however something about the way the sheep would squeal made me shiver. I remember everyone worked on the Golden Farm from sun up to sun down. All of the Grizzell cousins loved to visit and we never lacked for anything when Aunt Jane was around.

When I was there, everyone went out of their way to make me feel at home, knowing I was homesick to return to my family. My cousin Nancy and I were the same age, so we spent the majority of our time together. I slept with Nancy in a room she shared with her sister Janell. It was crowded, but warm. Nancy smiled a lot, like Aunt Jane, and we were all a happy crew. In Aunt Jane's bedroom, Nancy and I would play dress-up, putting on my aunt's old hats and clothes, and wearing "pop beads" around our necks. Afterwards, we would run outside in the fruit orchards, and sometimes we hid there hoping to get out of doing our share of the work. The orchards were full of ripe Granny Smith apples, peaches, pears and lots of plums. It was heavenly to reach right up and pick a piece of fruit off a tree, and then chomp down on it with a big, juicy bite. I thought to myself that an orchard would be perfect to have at our new house, wherever that was going to be.

Their big, weathered barn was the scene for some memorable events when I was there that summer, like the time Aunt Faye's daughter, Shirley, stuck a pitch fork through her sister's heel. It was an accident, of course, but everyone who witnessed it said the same thing, "I have never seen so much blood in my life!" Many of my cousins were there when it happened. Shirley picked up the pitchfork and dug it into a mound of hay to move it, but the fork slid across some slick manure and with amazing force, pierced into her sister's heel on the way up. Blood was spurting everywhere and Shirley, who was a teenager at the time, started screaming for help as loud as she could. Being the daughter of a nurse, she knew she needed the assistance of an adult as soon as possible, and she proceeded to leap up and over a five-foot-high section of fence to get help. Thankfully, Uncle Ward was close by tending to his honey bees. After a visit to the hospital in my uncle's Buick, everyone was relieved to learn no permanent damage had occurred. The pitchfork apparently barely missed her Achilles tendon.

One day, my cousin Jerry, who was probably about 15 years old, was climbing a ladder in the barn not realizing there was manure on the soles of his shoes. (There was a lot of manure on this farm!) He was almost at the top of the ladder when his foot slipped causing him to topple down several feet before his "heinie" landed firmly on the rim of a milk bucket. SLAM! OUCH! I did not see Jerry fall, but I was there when he had to sit in a washtub filled with warm, medicated water to heal his backside properly. He had to soak several times a day, it was very embarrassing! The only water at the house came from a deep well just outside the back door. I remember that was the coldest water I ever drank in my life! Aunt Jane would have to heat the water over an open fire to warm it for Jerry's soaks. I felt so bad for him, but over time it has made for a funny family story.

The most incredible of the family stories has been told for many years by reliable sources as the honest truth. It seems that the family farm house was in a frightful storm one day long ago. I always wondered why the front door was in the back of the house and the back door looked out toward the main road. The story has it that the house was picked up off its foundation and turned around during a tornado, landing almost perfectly perched as it was, only now backwards! Some stories are too crazy not to be true. Today, the turned-around house where Aunt Jane and Uncle Ward raised their children has been converted to an antique store by my cousin, Janell. It is fittingly named Golden Oldies. I can never go into that house without reliving many wonderful memories.

The Womack Farm, where Mo and Gee were staying, was run by my Aunt Dorothy, another of my father's sisters, and Uncle Wilson. Their dairy farm spread over a few hundred acres and was about three miles from the Golden Farm. Aunt Dorothy was a teacher in a one-room schoolhouse and Uncle Wilson ran the farm. Of course, a big farm necessitated everybody pitching in and working long, hard hours. Besides the heads of cattle, Uncle Wilson also raised hogs and chickens. The cows were milked by hand in the wee hours of the morning and again late in the evening. Attending to their gigantic, several-acre garden kept the younger cousins busy every waking hour. Mo and Gee were welcomed additions as they were expected to pitch-in each day until the work was done. The entire family worked tirelessly around the clock.

As with myself, my brothers were homesick on the farm for the rest of us. Once, Mo and Gee ran away, but did not get far. They climbed a tree in Aunt Dorothy's front yard, not realizing how easily they could be spotted. So that it wasn't all work for my brothers, Uncle Wilson let them try their hand at riding the hogs, which was risky business as the hogs were stubborn animals. This was never proven to be more true than when one of the hogs almost took my uncle's leg off several years later. The attack was brutal and he barely survived it. He was ill for the longest time and infection set in, which prolonged his recuperation. The injury left him with a limp, but it did not slow him down. My Uncle Wilson, like all of my aunts and uncles on the farm, had an unyielding work ethic.

My brothers and I loved the days we spent in the country with our Grizzell cousins: Don, Jeff, Jerry, Janell, Nancy, Freida, Penny, Lynette, Burnadette, Elvis, Lamar, Dwight, Kenneth and Ricky. Each in their own way made everything seem alright, no matter how down we were on our luck. Because of my wonderful extended family, I was the happiest kid in the world.

{ Nine }

LIVE OAK ROAD

I SAW MO grab Gee by the arm and with one continuous motion, he jerked our brother out of the room. There was a lot of commotion and yelling going on. My eyes focused on our leaky, wet ceiling just in time to witness several large cracks originate around the perimeter and simultaneously snake toward the mid-section. The ceiling was falling! It protruded downward with one huge bulge just before it cracked opened, dropping enough moisture-saturated insulation to fill the entire room. It sounded like thunder!

The insulation splashed everywhere. Holy cow! Gee could have been killed! Mo saved his life! Every time it rained, the ceiling leaked. But now, it had rained for days and we were oblivious to how much water had collected in the attic over the living room. What a mess! We could not begin to try to clean it all up. I remember one of my brothers saying, "Oh well, we probably will not live here that long anyway."

Mother, my siblings and I had all been separated from each other during the summer months and now, finally, my family was back together. We were as happy as could be when we moved to a two-bedroom rental house on Live Oak Road in Nashville, a few days before I started third grade in the fall. Not long after we were all reunited, my father reappeared. Many times, when he walked in the front door, I would ask him where he had been. I always got a crazy answer. He would tell me he was in a submarine testing atomic bombs or that he was on a secret government mission involving radiation. Once, he said he had a fish bone stuck in his throat and went to a special hospital in Idaho. My father had a skin condition, so he most often told me he was at a beach somewhere clearing up his psoriasis. At some point, I stopped asking the question.

My parents had a memorable altercation during this time; an incident which I will never forget. Burned into my brain is the vision of my father as he stood just outside the back door with a look of horror on his face, blinking through dozens of teeny particles of flying wood. The culprit? His prized fiddle. My petite, five-feet-two-inch Mother had splintered the fiddle over his head! Her small but mighty frame was in high gear as she reared back with his favorite instrument, slamming it over his head with hurricane force. She was so angry, she was literally speechless.

Our home was a lot of things, but it was not a violent home. However, my mother returned home from work that afternoon and discovered her sewing machine had been sold at a pawn shop. It was not unusual for household items to find their way to a pawn shop, but my father crossed a line by taking her portable Singer Sewing Machine. Mother had been commissioned to complete several articles of clothing for which she had been partially paid. She knew she must keep her word and make good on the promise to deliver the product. The machine also helped Mother from having to make all of our clothes entirely by hand (of which she was perfectly capable). She always had a thimble on her finger, creating new garments for us. Today, a seamstress has access to sewing machine attachments specifically designed for whipping up a button hole. Mother made them by hand and with precise measurements.

I do not remember how she managed to solve the problem of losing her machine, however it made for a great story. At the time, it was not the least bit humorous, but it still makes me laugh to picture Mother as she took revenge. My father was quite fond of playing that fiddle and quite talented, I might add. "We'll see how well you can honky-tonk now!" she scolded him. He was just as crippled to lose that fiddle as Mother was to lose her sewing machine. In a way, it was humorous to witness that small woman conquer a strong, broad shouldered, six-foot-two-inch man. Who would ever believe a common violin could double as a lethal weapon?!

Halloween night was always a big deal with us kids and could be enjoyed with little or no expense. That year, Mo took Gee and I trick-or-treating and helped us make our costumes. Mine was a tattered old white sheet which transformed me into a ghost. Gee dressed up like a vampire, his hair slicked back with Johnson's Baby Oil and a large piece of satin fabric became his cape. Mo smeared a bit of catsup on his face to imitate blood stains. Gee made a dashing Count Dracula! I recall the three of us collecting loads of candies. Our paper grocery bags were full to their brims when a group of boys passed us in a slow-moving car. I remember Mo using his body as a human shield to protect Gee and myself from the raw eggs the boys were tossing at us.

The winter temperatures were especially cold that year. Mo and Gee slept in the laundry room of our house. Of course, we had no laundry appliances, still the small room was equipped with a special outlet and a round hole in the wall where a dryer vent could be housed. The room was barely large enough for their black wrought-iron bunk beds. My brothers were so cold in that little space. Mother covered them with as many blankets and articles of clothing as she could find, clean or dirty, for warmth. As for the dryer vent hole which led outside, the boys stuffed it with bobby socks to prevent the chilly wind from coming inside. The linoleum floor was icy cold as if it was outdoors. Somehow, Elaine and I were always given the warmest and best room. We shared a rollaway bed for as long as I can remember. It was not as small as a twin-sized mattress, yet not as large as a full-sized mattress. The mattress was very thin and probably filled with straw. Although Mother struggled to keep our mattress odor fresh by sprinkling it with baking soda or baby powder, I peed on Elaine each night until I was at least thirteen years old.

Something happened that spring which really stunned us, leaving us with a feeling as if we were in the "Twilight Zone." Our father was entrepreneurial, trying his hand at a number of different careers. He and another man started a delivery service. I cannot recall that it was ever successful, however they had a few planning meetings in our living room (prior to the ceiling falling). They called the business B & G Delivery Service. My father's business partner's last name began with "B," and of course, the "G" stood for Grizzell. The man lived quite a distance from our house on Live Oak Road. He made it abundantly clear how much he missed his own child, an adolescent son, who had disappeared with his mother years earlier. He often described his frustrations regarding not knowing the whereabouts of his child. The heartbreak caused by the absence of his son seemed to consume him.

One evening just before dark, my brothers were playing catch in the front yard. Although they never owned ball gloves of their own, the other kids in the neighborhood provided enough balls and gloves for all the kids to participate. My father's business partner was casually looking out the window when suddenly he jumped up and ran out the storm glass door–his son was among the children who were playing in our yard. As it turned out, the boy lived a few houses away. I do not know the circumstances of why that family was separated. I only know the father and son were ecstatic to be reunited. What a coincidence!

As for me, there was one sweet girl in the neighborhood about my age. She was a beautiful Asian girl. I was in her home a few times and her family seemed very proper. They were bilingual and spoke often in their native language, which I could not understand. Funny how some memories last a lifetime, such as one I have about this young girl and I. We had been playing in the neighborhood, climbing trees and playing hide-and-seek with some other kids. Before we knew it, darkness fell so we had to hurry home as neither of us were allowed out after dark. I must have been nine or ten years old. I had to urinate really bad, so I stepped behind a bush where nobody could see me and peed on the ground. My Asian friend was mortified! She told me she would never be allowed to play with me again since I committed such an indecent act. All the while, I wondered what the big deal was? After all, I was used to outhouses and had stayed plenty of places where there was no bathroom. I thought as long as my privacy was protected by the bush, I was golden! Truthfully, it always bothered me and embarrassed me to have upset my friend to that degree.

We were evicted from the house on Live Oak Road soon after the ceiling fell. My father had vanished again and we were forced to vacate for non-payment of rent. When we left, we had no where to go. We scampered out without much more than the clothes on our backs and a few boxes of items. When we vacated, the ceiling remained just as it was the day it fell! I never saw my friend again, and I never knew what became of the man and his boy whose last names began with the letter "B."

{ Ten }

WEST END AVENUE

HOMELESS. WE WERE truly homeless. Thank goodness for two sets of grandparents, thirty-plus aunts and uncles and over sixty first cousins who loved us and were there for us when we had no roof over our heads. Granddaddy and Mommy Hale, our maternal grandparents, welcomed the six of us into their small home on West End Avenue in McMinnville, Tennessee, after we were evicted. Live Oak Road was the last of the three places we lived in Nashville. Although I am not certain of the time span, I believe we were in Nashville for less than three years.

It was a two-hour drive in Granddad Grizzell's old pickup truck to McMinnville. As usual, this was our only "cost-free" means of moving. It was always so embarrassing to be riding in the back of the old truck for the whole world to see. Up front in the cab, there was barely room for Mother, John Chris, some of our clothes and Granddad, who was behind the steering wheel and shifting the gears. We often wondered to ourselves how long that old truck could keep going.

In McMinnville, the center of activity was Main Street, which was lined with brick storefronts and popular merchants. There was McCrory's Five and Dime, Crouch's Drug Store, Cook's Department Store, a couple of hardware stores and of course, a feed-and-grain store. The Warren County Courthouse was built a couple of blocks from Main Street, located in the center of the old town square. McMinnville was once one of the top apple brandy producers in the nation due to its many apple orchards. Later, a thriving nursery industry developed with over 350 businesses still in operation today. Warren County is known as the "Nursery Capital of the World." Residents whose livelihood depends upon growing plants fare extremely well due to the rich, fertile soil. In the 1950s and 1960s, companies such as Oster, Century Electric, Formfit Rogers Lingerie and Genesco Shoe Factory provided additional jobs in the area.

Every year, the Warren County Agricultural and Livestock Fair takes place at the fairgrounds. In fact, the fair has been a tradition for over eighty years there. People come from all over to participate in contests or simply enjoy the festivities. At night, the carnival sounds of the midway echo throughout the fairgrounds. When we first moved to town, my Aunt Jane helped me prepare for a cooking contest at the fair as a member of the 4-H Club. The club always encouraged kids to participate in one event or another, whether it was raising a prize pig or growing the best tomatoes. I won a third-place ribbon for making deviled eggs. Aunt Jane taught me her special recipe using a little mustard and dill. These kinds of activities are at the heart of Warren County, where dedication to friends, neighbors and family are strengthened through community events, such as the fair. I am certain this is the case for many small towns, but McMinnville residents seem to have mastered the art.

Both sets of my Grandparents were born and raised in Warren County, and they remained there to marry and raise families of their own. Though Granddad Grizzell and Granddaddy Hale were very different men, they shared the same core values and work ethic. I can say with tremendous pride they were well respected in the community, both were hard-working family men and each above reproach. At different times, we lived with both sets of grandparents, but on this occasion Granddad Grizzell delivered us to Granddaddy Hale's house, where we would live for the next three or four months.

When Mother, Elaine, Mo, Gee, John Chris and I moved in with our Hale Grandparents, the house became quite crowded. Mother's youngest siblings, my Aunt June and Uncle Tim, still lived at home, which meant there were ten of us in a small, four-room house. June was a beautiful, young woman in her twenties, who I thought looked like a movie star. June treated me like royalty, always combing my hair and making a fuss over me. Tim was only slightly older than me. It seemed strange for Elaine and Mo to have an uncle younger than they were.

We ate lots of biscuits with red-eye gravy there. Red-eye gravy was never my favorite, but plentiful because the ingredients were easy to obtain. Red-eye gravy was simply drippings from country ham or bacon, mixed with coffee grounds. Mommy

Hale made a big pot of pinto beans and cornbread everyday. The cornbread was fried in small portions like pancakes. We called them hoecakes. Yum! When I was a child, I wondered why they were called hoecakes. According to the *Oxford English Dictionary*, the term "hoecake" was used by American writers as early as 1745. The origin of the name actually refers to the method of preparation: field hands often cooked them on a shovel, or hoe, held to an open flame. Hoes designed for cotton fields were large and flat with a hole for the large handle to slide through; the blade could be removed and placed over a fire much like a griddle.

The Hale house had no bathroom. The outhouse had a single seat (most of the ones I had been in had double seats). You could always count on having a Sears & Roebuck or J.C. Penney catalog which doubled as toilet paper. We were coached about being thrifty rather than wasteful with the number of pages we tore out of the books. Not only did we need to ration the pages to accommodate the entire family, the soiled pages were dropped in the outhouse hole and were not exactly considered biodegradable. There was much to consider when families did not have simple conveniences, such as indoor plumbing.

My Granddaddy, William Nathan Hale, worked hard every day as a carpenter. His handiwork could be seen in so many of the structures in McMinnville. Granddaddy was a perfectionist when it came to building things. Most evenings, he could be found whittling on the front porch after supper. He whittled miniature plows, tractors and other farm equipment, usually from cedar wood. I enjoy the familiar smell of cedar today because it reminds me of him. He cherished the small things in life and was a master at making us laugh. He was the only person who called me "Polly," instead of Paula.

My Hale grandparents had seen more than their share of hardships. When Granddaddy married Mommy Hale, he was 39 years old and she was 17 years old. He was a tall, lean and handsome widower who lost his first wife and one of their five children to rheumatic fever, for which there was no cure. Another of the five children died on Granddaddy's shoulder as he was transporting the child via train after the little boy had been kicked in the head by a spooked pony. Granddaddy told me the story once, with a shaky voice and tears flowing, about how he wrapped a pillow case around the child's head in an attempt to prevent the boy's exposed brain from falling out of his skull. Needless to say, his precious son stopped breathing before my Granddaddy could get him to a hospital some seventy miles from home.

Not long afterwards, a distant relative introduced Granddaddy to Mary Pauline Cooley, who became his wife. She was a well-respected young lady who married to care for a man and his three remaining children, which was so common in the early 1900s. Although my mother was Granddaddy's sixth child, she was the oldest of seven children my maternal grandparents had together. Counting the children from both of his wives, Granddaddy Hale had twelve children. I have never met anyone since I was a little girl who loved children and babies as much as Granddaddy Hale. When my mother was born, her step brother and sisters were teenagers. From what I have heard, they considered her a baby doll. She loved them dearly her entire life and they returned her love a million times over.

Mommy Hale was a beautiful, petite woman. Though only a teenager, she watched over children Willette, Ed and Inez the best she knew how. My Aunt Willette taught Mommy Hale how to cook red-eye gravy. After my mother was born, Mommy Hale gave birth to John Leroy, Jane Ann, Hallie June (everyone called her June), Fred Louis, Nathan and lastly, Tim. Unfortunately, my grandparents lost Mother's little brother, Fred Louis, when the boy was an adolescent. All I remember from the stories was that he had spinal meningitis and died suddenly. He was described as a gentle, loving, obedient child whom everyone adored. How fitting for Gee to be named after Fred Louis: Gary Louis Grizzell. I guess Gee was my mother's tribute to the baby brother she lost.

Like my mother, Mommy Hale could sew like nobody's business. People always said she could make "anything from nothing." She made dozens of adorable sock-monkey dolls over the years for us to play with. Mommy Hale had a Singer Treadle Sewing Machine, which was operated by a foot petal and required no electricity. My mother was a whiz with that machine. She enjoyed being able to get exercise at the same time she made a garment. Mother clearly inherited her talents as a seamstress from Mommy Hale. I am proud to have been named after my grandmother, Pauline Hale.

The months at West End Avenue flew by. We ate the same foods everyday. But, we had food on the table everyday! We slept on the floor, but we did not care. I had no idea we were having such a hard time financially. Per her usual tactics, Mother worked hard to keep our minds busy while living in that small house. She used every opportunity as a teaching avenue, such as telling us about the colorful, blooming plants and bushes in the yard or constantly giving us things to think about. Although Mother helped us in every way she could, it broke her heart to know Mo had to pretend to have forgotten his baseball glove when he played in the neighborhood or that I had to pretend to have forgotten my notebook paper when at school. Even with all of the hardships, she made it seem like we were the happiest family on the face of the earth.

I truly was as happy as I could be, that is, until I was bitten by a dog the size of a small pony. I was standing in Granddaddy's yard minding my own business, when a huge mutt calmly walked up to me and proceeded to bite the calf of my leg. As Forrest Gump might have said, "that dog bit me for no particular reason at all."

{ Eleven }

SEITZ STREET

MUCH OF THE time we lived on Seitz Street in McMinnville was a blur. I don't recall Mother or John Chris being in the house at all. It was a ridiculous excuse for a house; a small, wood-framed structure with virtually no insulation. We could see daylight through the cracks in the dilapidated walls. The house was literally leaning to one side, making me fear it would fall over any minute. There were two bedrooms which were devoid of furniture, so we slept on the floor. Our beds were made from piles of clothing, sheets and quilts, all stacked on top of one another.

On "lucky" days, one of my aunts or uncles would drop off garden vegetables or homegrown fruits. This held true every place we lived. We never went to a doctor unless we were sick. We never went to a dentist unless we had a toothache. I remember Uncle John Leroy taking me to a dentist because I had a bad toothache and a very swollen jaw. The dentist pulled my tooth. My uncle pulled out his wallet and paid the dentist as we left the office. Too bad I was in so much pain from the toothache, otherwise I would have considered myself lucky to go for a drive with Uncle John Leroy. I always looked forward to the times we got to play with his children: Hoyt, Terri, Debbie and Missy.

When I think of Seitz Street, I think of a true story which taught me several valuable lessons. On this particular day, Gee and I were home alone with Mo. We were genuinely hungry. I recall the pain in my gut as it begged for nutrients. The hunger pangs were mild compared to the pain of witnessing Gee and Mo's hunger. I loved my siblings so deeply, I could not bear to see them lacking for anything. My guess is I was almost ten years old, which meant Mo was thirteen at the most. He felt responsible for our well-being and set out to find a way to feed us.

There was a big blackberry patch within walking distance of the house. Mo made us put on long sleeved shirts to protect us from chiggers. It seemed as though blackberry patches were breeding grounds for chiggers and ticks. Gee and I reluctantly followed Mo to the berry patch, grumbling the whole way. We all carried empty one-gallon sorghum syrup buckets. After picking berries for what seemed like a lifetime, we started back home. Gee's cheeks and mouth were purple from the berries he had sampled.

I despised picking berries. Partly, because I was afraid of snakes and undoubtedly would see a couple on each berry-picking excursion. They were harmless, but I hated snakes nonetheless. Once when we were picking berries at the Grizzell Farm, we saw a snake hanging from a tree overhead. The other reason I despised the blackberry patch was it usually resulted in a bout with poison oak or poison ivy. Mommy Hale's remedy for poison oak and poison ivy was Glyco. Yuk! It is a reddish, liquid potion which smells exactly like the Listerine Aunt Faye gargled with everyday. I may not have cared for the odor of Glyco, but it effectively lessened the horrible itching poison ivy caused. Mother also rubbed Glyco on Elaine's gums due to frequent inflammation. Glyco seemed to remedy most any ailment.

When we arrived back at the house from our berry picking spree, Gee showed excitement as any child would; obviously thinking we would have a berry feast. Mo snatched the berries from us. As he walked to a neighbor's yard, he told us to wait for him. He borrowed the neighbor's garden hose in order to clean the berries, since the water had been turned off in our house due to delinquent payments. Then, he explained we would not be eating the berries, for he was planning to sell them. As a result of the three of us picking berries, Mo was able to fill two one-gallon buckets with plump, fresh, tasty blackberries. I sometimes think of Mo as the entrepreneur of my childhood because he only had to knock on two doors to sell both gallons for $1 each. With the two dollars, he walked to the nearby store and returned home with a loaf of Colonial white bread and a quart of Mayfield Farms milk.

We had a large jar of peanut butter that we scraped over and over as we tried to get out all of its contents. Funny how many times we would go back to the same seemingly empty jar and scrape out enough for one more bite. That was the day I realized my brother Mo was a genius. Gee and I were eagerly waiting for our portions of milk and bread. We waited and watched as Mo scraped that big Peter Pan peanut butter jar. He handed each of us a half sandwich and a glass of milk. Gee began to cry because he thought Mo would not have a sandwich. Mo wrapped a dishtowel around the jar and strategically slammed it on the edge of the hard countertop. He carefully opened the dishtowel allowing the large pieces of the peanut butter jar to fall into the towel. We watched as he scraped the rounded section of the bottom of the jar which allowed him to retrieve peanut butter which could not be reached when the jar was intact. Genius! Who would have thought? Indeed, there was enough for another half sandwich.

Mo does not remember that day, however I find it compelling each time I think about it. What I remember as clearly as the broken jar episode was the warning he gave Gee and myself. He made us promise we would never try to duplicate his stunt, fearing we would cut ourselves.

I cannot recall how long we lived on Seitz Street, just that it was not during the time school was in session. When I think of that time period, I remain puzzled about where Mother and John Chris were. My father was not at this house, ever. I think of how the little house leaned to one side, as if it were going to go crashing down at any moment. Most of all, I think of Mo, the blackberries and the peanut butter jar.

{ Twelve }

SPRING STREET

A TALL, GOOD-LOOKING man came to our shabby house on Spring Street in McMinnville. He walked past the old tires and the tacky yard art that decorated our front yard, items we inherited when we moved in. The house sat very close to the road and the front porch was level with the ground. We could hear the man's footsteps as he walked across the wooden porch planks. Mother answered the door, but did not invite the man in. She leaned on the door frame with the storm door partially opened. Her body language was courteous, but not inviting. As he left, I heard Mother thanking him for his time, acknowledging the fact that he was looking out for our best interest.

The man was a truant officer and I can remember on more than one occasion when an official would visit us at our house. I'm sure they would have visited more often if they could have kept up with us. I seriously doubt Mother registered our new address with the school or the post office when we moved. With each visit, Mother listened carefully and spoke very professionally. She never lied and she always said she expected things to improve for us financially. Mother stood proud and tall, never flinching at the questions thrown her way. She was the mother hen and that was that. Remarkably, she was always able to hide the fact that the electricity may have been turned off or that we had no running water in the house.

Our Spring Street house was a small, two-bedroom dwelling located next to a cemetery. I don't like graveyards and living so near to one was less than thrilling. In the moonlight, the tombstones were downright spooky across from our small, frame house. Although acres and acres of cemetery made for a perfect place to run around, in hindsight, playing amongst the tombstones was certainly disrespectful. When we moved in, the black wrought-iron bunk and rollaway beds mysteriously reappeared. Somehow, a handful of our furniture items had found us, though they were not at our last location. I was perplexed. Over the last few months, where were the bunks beds stored? Typically, we moved without notice and were unable to carry many belongings with us. We would start all over again, acquiring socks, underwear and the bare necessities.

The house had steep outdoor steps in the back which led to a dark basement with a dirt floor. There was a wringer washing machine in the basement which was operated by a hand-crank, requiring no electricity. There was just one problem: no water in the basement. Mother washed our clothes by hand in the kitchen sink with lye soap. She washed clothes each and every day, hanging them on a clothes line in the yard. She worked very hard at keeping our things fresh and clean.

When we had no water, things became more difficult. Mother would clean our clothes at Mommy Hale's house or by using water, with permission, from a neighbor's well or hose. During these times, I was absent from school more than I was present. Mother was not ignorant to the importance of education. However, I am convinced she had to weigh the effects of us going to school without the ability to bathe properly. She was tremendously concerned about how our peers viewed us and she was not willing to send us to school in a condition in which we would be ridiculed. I remember so well how Mother would spit on the corner of her apron to clean a dirty spot on my face. Nobody left the house without Mother putting us in our best and cleanest clothes, even if that meant wearing the same thing several days in a row, which was plenty normal. I believe this is why Mother furiously worked to sew us new clothes. Honestly, I think it was easier for her to sew a new shirt than it was to wash a soiled one by hand, dry it on the line and then iron it. She reused fabric and buttons all of the time, never wasting anything that could be recycled. She would tear out an old zipper and put it in a new garment in the blink of an eye. When you think about it, our clothes were always brand new and tailor made.

The day after we moved in, Aunt Dixie drove up with my cousins Debbie and Terri. Aunt Dixie and Uncle John Leroy, my mother's brother, were always willing to share whatever their family possessed. I remember the baby blue car coat she brought which was just my size. Even though it was a hand-me-down, it was just perfect. I loved the white furry edge around the hood. She gave Elaine a pair of slippers similar to ballerina shoes. My cousin Hoyt was barely bigger than Gee, which meant Gee often was given his clothes when he outgrew them. Debbie was a little taller than me, making me the beneficiary of her things. I distinctly remember them sharing with us, often relinquishing clothes they could still wear. I loved being around Aunt Dixie. She and Mother always made each other laugh. They laughed about everything. I remember how they sat with a big batch of green beans in their laps, snapping them in preparation for cooking. The green beans were called white half runners; add warm cornbread and we had a meal fit for kings.

Mother entertained Debbie, Terri, Gee, John Chris and myself with a game of "Hide the Thimble." John Chris, who was no more than five years old, would grab the thimble and run behind Mother for safety. He was as cute as a button with his red curls and he made Mother laugh when he disrupted the game. Mother was ingenious when it came to creating inexpensive ways to keep her children occupied. I will never forget how she made her thimble into Thumbelina. Imagine that in a few short minutes she could crochet a teeny ruffled dress, which transformed an old tarnished thimble into a little finger puppet. Mother's thimbles served in multiple capacities. Her thimble became a baby's medicine cup when needed. Her thimble protected her small, rough hands when she made all those little socks, shirts and skirts for us. Mother's thimble was as much a part of her hand as her fingers.

Mother had no formal education other than that of a

nursing assistant. She was an avid reader. She especially loved to read about history and geography, although she read anything she could get her hands on. She educated herself through her readings to the point where it seemed she knew something about everything. After we all left home, she became a crossword puzzle expert. She would *become* whatever she was reading about, especially when she was enjoying *National Geographic* or *Reader's Digest*. Those publications were her great escape from life's harsh realities. Mother was diligent about insisting her children utilize the public libraries; not just because we didn't have encyclopedias or other books at home, but because she knew the value of education. She reasoned this was an affordable way to gain information and grow academically.

She was also an excellent disciplinarian. Mother did not hesitate to wash our mouths out with Ivory soap whenever we said a bad word or anything disrespectful. Trust me, Mother's Ivory soap was an unforgettable punishment. She also had a switch that she would use on us whenever we disrespected her or another human being. Mother was only five-feet two-inches tall, but you would never know that by the way she kept her children in line. Funny thing is, the shortest of her five children is five-feet seven-inches tall (me). Mother was stern when she needed to be, but she was always fair. I truly believe I got more switching than anybody else. My siblings jest that I got a switching every day of my life. To tell the truth, I think I just got caught more than the others. Whether it was climbing a dangerous tree or staying out past curfew, I never got away with anything. My father never spanked me. He saved the real lashings for my brothers, whether they needed it or not...that was the way I saw it anyway.

After I was grown, I learned when Mother was switching our legs she was switching her own at the same time, to ensure she never popped us too hard. She never crossed the line into physical abuse that many parents do, much to their children's detriment. However, she definitely believed in spankings.

Our stay in the house on Spring Street was brief but memorable. The Godwin family lived behind us. Bud Godwin was a local radio personality and well-liked by his audience. I think he and Mrs. Godwin had six children. It seems between our family and the Godwin family there were almost a dozen kids running around. We had a grand time playing in the backyard. In my mind, we lived next to a celebrity: Mr. Bud Godwin, famous Warren County radio personality!

One day after school, one of the Godwin boys came tearing over to our house to tell us the president had been shot. We had no television or radio of our own, so Mother, Gee, John Chris and I went to the Godwin's front porch to listen to the radio announcements. This was one of the most tragic news stories of our lifetime and we almost had no way of knowing about it. At age eleven, I was still too young to understand the enormous impact this event had on our country. However, I could see that Mother was devastated. Our world seemed to stop for a few days as we mourned President Kennedy. A quiet, somber eeriness hovered around us like a fog.

Out of the blue one evening at bedtime, Mother was

tucking us in and exclaimed, "Children, tomorrow we are moving to a nicer place." Unbelievably, we were moving into a brand-new house with brand-new furniture. No more broken appliances. No more old tires and tacky yard art. And no more run-down houses. Finally, things were going our way.

{ Thirteen }

MARGO LANE

TWO MEN DRESSED in matching blue jumpsuits knocked on the front door. They politely pushed their way past Elaine, picked up our furniture one piece at a time, carried each into a large moving van and drove away. Our new furniture had been repossessed. Repossessed!

Moving to Margo Lane was ludicrous! For the life of me, I will never understand how we managed to move into a new, three-bedroom ranch-style house in a new neighborhood. It was a joke; but it was not funny. However, it was wonderful to have indoor plumbing in perfect working condition. The toilet actually flushed! Many of the houses we lived in had a bathroom, but they often housed broken toilets or toilets with no running water.

We moved in Granddad Grizzell's old truck, as we had so many times before. I began to realize the only times we piled into that old truck together was on moving day, with Mother and John Chris in the cab with Granddad, and the rest of us in the back with our beds, trying to keep what few clothes we had with us from flying out with the wind. The sound of the popping clutch was magnified when heard from the truck bed, resonating all around us.

By some miracle, we had a new living room sofa and chair, plus, a new dining table with six matching chairs at Margo Lane. Even though we had electric heat, the house felt cold, probably due to the bare hardwood floors and windows with no draperies. In no time, Mother had stitched together curtains, hanging them on dowel rods which doubled as curtain rods. I watched as she ripped the seams out of a burlap sack and laid it on the floor. With a thimble protecting her finger, she cut the fabric in half, sewed a hem at the bottom and stitched the top just right, in order to hang it in the single window over the kitchen sink. She tied colorful ribbons on each side making the shape of two "R"s, one facing the other. My mother was an amazing seamstress. The way she utilized her resources was remarkable.

Mother did not work outside the home when we lived in McMinnville. In addition to her sewing and crocheting jobs, she made baseballs in our living room with a kit that came by mail order. Mother worked with a wooden device that looked like a giant clothespin standing upright. The unit held a tightly-wound ball of string as Mother sewed on the leather baseball skin with leather thread. It was a very hard job and we all helped her when we could. When the baseballs were all made, Mother mailed them back and got paid. My brothers never had a real baseball to play with, but there was often a big bag full of brand-new baseballs sitting in our living room.

Our new house felt like home. The black wrought-iron bunk beds were in my brother's room, my sister and I had the rollaway bed, and Aunt Dixie gave Mother a full-sized bed for her room. There were no chests with drawers, but we did not care. Mother was so proud of our new house that she invited the truant officer to come back and see us. This time she greeted the man at the door with a smile on her face and invited him in to sit at our new kitchen table. She offered him sweet tea and peanut butter fudge. She was hospitable and charming, and she personally promised to ensure that our schoolwork would not suffer.

Like the rest of us, my sister Elaine worked a number of part-time jobs while in high school. She was working long hours at McCrory's Five-and-Dime on Main Street in McMinnville and we saw very little of her. She brought gumdrops and double-dipped, chocolate-covered peanuts home to us from time to time. If I remember correctly, the owner of the store allowed Elaine to eat for free at the soda fountain. Free food was probably the most important benefit of her job. For a while, she worked at Crouch's Drug Store as a clerk, and she also worked at Formfit Rogers Lingerie, a factory that specialized in women's lingerie. It was hard for her because she always had to hitch a ride or go to work by taxicab. Try traveling by taxi with no home telephone!

When Elaine was a junior at Central High, it came time to order high school rings. It was only natural that she dreamed of having one. However, it was out of the question that Mother would be able to afford the cost of a ring. Our Uncle Isaac John had a daughter, Freida, the same age as Elaine. He was keenly aware of the importance this memento held to a high school student. He surprised Elaine by ordering her a Central High class ring, dated the year she would graduate. In the center of the ring was an emerald, her birthstone. Her hand looked beautiful adorned with that ring. At school, Elaine often had the highest grade point average of any girl in her class. As a result, she was voted "most likely to succeed" and was pictured in her senior yearbook sitting in a wheelbarrow filled with cash. How ironic that one of us Grizzell kids would be surrounded by so much cash! We were all proud of Elaine when she graduated, but Mother was simply glowing.

How well I remember thinking our luck had changed for the better. We were safe and warm in our new home. We were together and we were happy. But I was missing my father. I was too young to understand that his frequent and lengthy disappearances were signs that he was leading a troubled life. My father was living in the shadows and was not honoring the promises he made, both to my mother and to the people he owed money. One day, Mother arranged to take me to visit my father in the Warren County Jail where he was being held after an arrest. The story I was told was that he had collected several large payments for landscaping jobs, but had not completed any of the work. At the jail, an officer escorted us to a dimly lit room with a concrete floor. The floor was gray and the walls were gray. My father came into the room and sat beside me on a metal bench. He was crying really hard with his face buried in his hands. It broke my heart to see him locked up. I was worried about him and I missed him. My father was incarcerated for short periods of time on several occasions. I remember several times when Uncle John Leroy tried to help him land on his feet. Sometimes, my father's brothers produced the bail money for his release. A debt, I'm sure, my father never repaid.

Not too long afterwards, I remember complaining to Mother that my neck hurt. I was only a little girl in Oak Ridge when doctors had first noticed a lump on my neck. Dr. Bigelow removed the benign tumor and everything was fine. Now, ten years later, Mother took me back to Dr. Bigelow. Since we never owned a car, Mother borrowed one from a neighbor and off we drove to Oak Ridge. This time was different, the doctor surmised. The tumor had grown back in the same place. Dr. Bigelow told my mother a large tumor had returned on my thyroid, but this time it was cancer. Mother questioned him, asking, "You mean, MAYBE it is cancer?" No, he declared, it was cancer and it was a bad cancer. He told my mother he would operate the following week to remove all he could, but chances were I would not survive very long.

None of us ever went anyplace alone with Mother. But this time, she and I spent the next several days driving around McMinnville and visiting each and every one of my aunts, uncles, grandparents and most of my first cousins. When we got to each house, we would share hugs and kisses, then Mother would say, "Paula Faye, run outside to play." I sized it up in a hurry and figured that I was not long for this world. Why else would my mother be taking me to all of these places?

Everybody gave me loads of presents! I mean, this was great! I got new pajamas, new baby dolls and stuffed animals galore. It was better than any Christmas, ever. We had a lot of food at our house. People from church brought food. Many of my aunts brought food. It was as if I had already died and gone to heaven. Soon, we packed up my new pajamas and dolls and we went back to Oak Ridge Hospital. Never will I forget the smell of the ether, which was used for anesthesia. Ugh! I can smell it still! When I woke up after surgery, my throat was sore and I could feel a huge bandage around my neck. As I opened my eyes, I noticed the guardrails were raised on my bed. I leapt up and over the guardrail landing flat-footed on the floor. Mother rose out of her chair in horror since Dr. Bigelow's instructions were not to allow me out of bed. Everyone was happy to learn it was a false alarm; no cancer. Mother held me in her arms and through her tears told me about the "power of prayer."

That year at Christmas, we celebrated with a real tree in a real metal stand. Mother crocheted more of her little white angels to hang on the tree. Each angel was perfectly shaped with little heads and little wings and little skirts. She also crocheted several stars with white thread. We hooked the crocheted items on the tree with paperclips. Mother lined the tree limbs with cotton to look just like snow. There were no lights on the tree, but no matter. The white angels and white stars and white cotton limbs made it glow in the dark. It was magical.

Mother was crocheting every waking minute. She

crocheted so fast she became seasick if she looked down at the motion of her own little hands. We were so accustomed to seeing bundles of thread in her lap, we did not realize she was crocheting our holiday gifts. She was making each of us afghans for our beds and matching house slippers. On Christmas Eve, Uncle John Leroy, Aunt Dixie and cousins Hoyt, Debbie, Teri and Missy came to visit. Mother made peanut butter fudge and everyone was happy. We played a killer game of Scrabble, which gave Mother and my uncle a perfect excuse to argue. Since they were born a year apart, Mother and Uncle John Leroy had plenty of experience arguing with one another. Talk about sibling rivalry, they wrote the book! It was amusing to witness the way they bickered considering how protective they were of one another. When my cousins went home, Mother gave them a box of dominoes as a Christmas present. I thought to myself, "We must be rich."

But soon, it was back to reality for Mother and us kids. I have no idea if Mother or someone else paid for my surgery. I'm sure we were soon out of money again. Just after Christmas, our wonderful new furniture was repossessed and right before New Year's, we were evicted.

{ Fourteen }

MIKE MUNCEY ROAD

DURING THE WINTER break from school, I went back to live with my mother's parents, Granddaddy and Mommy Hale. They had recently moved to a modest, small home near McMinnville on Mike Muncey Road. My family was having a particularly hard time making ends meet, so it was necessary for us to split up again. When I lived with my grandparents, I attended 7th grade at Dibrell High School.

My Granddaddy had recently retired, so my Uncle Nathan helped him and Mommy Hale buy a two-bedroom house and move it to the farm property of my Aunt Jane Ann and Uncle Carl. My grandparents' house was placed across a pasture from Aunt Jane Ann's house and next to one of their big horse barns. It was far enough away for privacy, yet close enough if they ever needed help. The house did not have a bathroom at first, only an outhouse in the back. At least it was a two-seater! As a kid, I always wondered why more than one seat was required. Why would anyone want to use the outhouse at the same time as someone else? I remember Mo peeing out in the pasture one time when he got quite a jolt from an electric fence. He was fine, but it sure was funny. A few years later, all of these bathroom problems were resolved: my grandparents had one built inside the house.

Aunt Jane Ann and Uncle Carl maintained a several-hundred acre farm where they raised all manner of livestock. They also cared for a huge garden which included every vegetable imaginable. The farm had cows, hogs, chickens and, most importantly, horses. Horses were Uncle Carl's specialty and he was once a renowned rodeo rider. He held several impressive national titles in roping, which was his passion. I never saw him without his cowboy hat and boots, and I often wondered if he wore his cowboy hat to bed. A rope circled on his belt was a regular part of his outfit when he worked with his livestock. Uncle Carl had a way with horses like nobody I had ever seen. He spoke to them in a whisper and looked them straight in the eye. He could tame a wild buck in no time, which he often did for friends and neighbors. If a horse looked me in the eye, all you would see of me is the back of my head as I went in the opposite direction. No sir, I was a city girl!

Although a very successful man, Uncle Carl had his share of bad luck. He served in the armed forces during World War II and fought in the "Battle of the Bulge." He badly injured his leg while in the service and he also suffered severe frost bite. For the remainder of his life, he had a stiff leg which caused a significant limp, but it never slowed him down. Unfortunately, Uncle Carl was involved in a serious farming accident years later.

He was harvesting a field of hay one day when his tractor turned over, landing on top of his bad leg. Uncle Carl was unconscious and trapped beneath one of the biggest tractors that John Deer ever manufactured. He was taken to the Veteran's Hospital in Nashville where it took many weeks for him to fully recover. In an effort to support my uncle, about a dozen of his neighbors transported their own tractors to the farm and worked tirelessly to harvest Uncle Carl's crops after the accident occurred. A picture of all those men on their tractors was featured on the front page of Warren County's newspaper, *The Standard*.

Aunt Jane Ann is one of Mother's younger sisters. In addition to her responsibilities of farming, she worked full-time at Genesco Shoe Factory for forty years. As luck would have it, her little feet were the perfect size for modeling sample shoes. She modeled shoes for Genesco and had opportunity to buy the latest fashions at discounted prices. Unfortunately, my foot was at least three sizes too big to get her hand-me-downs. Aunt Jane Ann bought clothes for me and my sister, Elaine, and on many occasions she helped my mother financially when times were tough. She taught me how to make white milk gravy, which my family will attest is the only dish I prepare well. Aunt Jane Ann remains a favorite, not just to me and my siblings, but to all the nieces and nephews.

My uncle, Timothy Winfred Hale, Mother's youngest brother, was born only two years before me and was still living at home when I moved in. Tim rode the bus to Dibrell High with me every day while I was there. He was the life of the party on the bus. The kids loved Tim because he was such a jokester, and everyone wanted to be near him. He cared little for studying, but was plenty bright. Tim was all about the social aspects of school. Wherever he was, laughter and joy followed, even his mannerisms were funny. All of us had southern accents, but Tim exaggerated his by saying "thare" instead of "there" and "diddy" instead of "daddy." He had a way of making each person feel as if they were the only person in the room.

Being with Tim and my Hale grandparents was a special treat since I had to be away from my siblings. My time at Dibrell High School was brief and uneventful. When the school year ended, I was reunited with my siblings. As much as I wanted to be with my family, I would miss the times I spent with my Uncle Tim as he had a way of making all of your troubles disappear.

A few years later, Tim was drafted into the Army. Everyone agrees Granddaddy Hale was never the same after watching his youngest child ship off to Vietnam. The entire family was devoted to writing to Tim whenever possible, having only limited knowledge regarding how rough things actually were in the war. He returned home, but never regained his health after sustaining multiple serious injuries.

Tim only shared his experiences with me personally on one occasion, which was on a Veteran's Day many years after he returned to the states. What I learned was that after the traditional basic training, he was assigned to the thickest part of the jungle. He told me he never felt prepared for the responsibilities placed upon him. "I was challenged to fire upon the enemy that we often could not see," he told me, "and I didn't understand why these men were considered my enemy. Many of them were simply scared kids."

Tim was injured twice. The first time, he was shot while carrying a wounded fellow soldier to safety. He recovered from this as the bullet only grazed his shoulder. Unfortunately, his next injury was a life-changing event. He sustained a major wound to his mid-section, leaving a gaping, exposed hole in his abdomen and rendering him immobile. Although his platoon was under heavy attack, a fellow soldier removed his own mud-soaked shirt, rolled it into a wad and stuffed it into Tim's abdomen in an effort to stop the bleeding. Tim was carried out of the jungle, just as he had carried the other soldier before him. Within a few weeks, he was flown to the Veteran's Hospital in Nashville where he began his recovery.

After his stint in the war, Tim was different in that he was nervous and startled easily. I observed how worried Granddaddy Hale was about his son and how Tim's active duty had changed him. As a teenager, Tim enjoyed hunting quail or rabbits, now he could not bear the sound of gunfire. It hurt my heart to see that my fun-loving uncle had become a troubled soul. I knew I would never understand what Tim endured, I just wished I could fix it for him. Tim spent many years in and out of the hospital, undergoing more than thirty surgeries. He was constantly in the company of friends and family who desired to be near him. Even on his worse day, he tried to make others laugh. Without a doubt, he made us thankful for our health. Tim married and had two lovely daughters, Shelly and Crystal, whom he was very proud of. Although my uncle never enjoyed a healthy body again, the memories he carried with him from the battlefield scarred him far worse than any bullet could. My Uncle Tim passed away at the young age of fifty-two. None of us were ready to lose him, especially his sweet daughters. He was truly a hero in everyone's eyes.

In addition to Tim, I am proud to have other military veterans in my family tree. My cousin Hoyt Hale was drafted into the army during the Vietnam era. Thankfully, his time was served in Germany rather than in combat. I love him for serving our country. Mother's cousin, Raymond H. Cooley, was a World War II veteran who was personally honored at the White House by President Harry S. Truman in 1946. During combat in the Philippines, Raymond threw himself on a grenade to protect the men in his unit. He was severely injured and lost his right hand in the explosion. In the crowded East Room, President Truman presented Raymond with the Medal of Honor, the nation's supreme award for valor. Today, a stretch of Highway 28 in Tennessee is named after Raymond in his honor.

My Uncle Carl, Uncle Tim, cousin Hoyt, and Mother's cousin Raymond gave and sacrificed so much for their country, as did all five of my father's brothers. Each man, in his own way, demonstrated a remarkable sense of duty, bravery and unselfishness.

{ Fifteen }

NUNLEY STREET

TWENTY-FIVE DOLLARS! Gee and I won twenty-five dollars. Our house on Nunley Street was a government-subsidized housing unit; dozens of duplexes standing high on a hilltop in West Riverside, a community in McMinnville. The duplex was new with freshly sown grass. The manager of the neighborhood offered prizes for the families with the prettiest yard when the project was a few weeks old. I am uncertain whether Gee and I did anything to promote the growth of the grass, but we won third place in the yard contest nonetheless. Twenty-five dollars was a small fortune to us.

Our brief stay on Nunley Street was unforgettable. This was where we lived when I experienced my first migraine headache at age 12. Little did I know I would be plagued with migraines for the remainder of my life. Hard as I tried, I could never forget that hot summer day. Mother made Gee and John Chris stay outside, rather than running in and out; preventing them from slamming the screen door. The least, little noise made my head feel as if it would burst. My vision was obstructed with colorful, squiggly lines intertwined with periods of foggy blurriness, and accompanied with numbness in my hands and fingertips. My speech was disrupted by my inability to formulate words properly. Each of these symptoms are the warnings signs of the migraine headache that follows, which comes like a jackhammer splitting your head in half. When the headaches happened at school, I would have to ask to lie down or get someone to take me home. Mother could not afford to take me to a doctor. The only thing worse than the pain of a migraine was the helpless look on the face of our dear mother. As time would tell, only an abscessed tooth or a lump in the neck warranted a visit to a doctor.

Although it did not seem like it at the time, Mo got one of the biggest breaks of his life as a teenager. Granddad Grizzell drove to see us one day, specifically to have a conversation with Mother. Granddad adored and respected Mother and would have done anything for her. He explained that Mr. Oliver Cook, the local clothes merchant, had approached him regarding an outstanding balance my father had at his store. My father had charged a new wardrobe for himself at this upscale store, and then pulled one of his disappearing acts. Granddad suggested Mo could work in the store to repay our father's debt, which totalled $360. The idea was fine with Mr. Cook, but Granddad's true agenda was to provide stability and experience for Mo. He knew Mo would make him proud.

But there was one small problem: Cook's Department Store would have to pass the Mary Ruth Grizzell test. Mother was not about to allow her son to work for people she did not know and at a place of business with which she was not familiar. When Granddad left that day, Mother used a neighbor's phone to call a taxi to drive Mo and herself to the department store. After meeting the owners, she checked with friends and family and determined they were fine, reputable people. Were they ever! They taught my brother many things and learned to love him like their own son.

In the beginning Mo worked only on Saturdays. His pay was $5.12 per day, half of which was applied to my father's debt. Mo was happy to have $2.56 each week. At first, his duties were limited to sweeping the floors and general cleaning. Pretty soon, he was given the task of steaming, folding and straightening shirts and slacks. Next, Mr. Cook encouraged Mo to buy a few clothes for himself because he had plans to use my brother on the sales floor. Mo learned to take meticulous care of his new clothes and he became a valued employee in record time.

Like Mother, Mo put his heart and soul into everything he did. If it was worth doing, it was worth doing well. It took Mo one year to pay off that $360 debt. He kept a makeshift spreadsheet as he went. The day the debt was cleared, Mo went to Mr. and Mrs. Cook and said, "My father's balance is zero, so I want to thank you for allowing me the opportunity to work here." Naturally, he thought since his mission was accomplished, he would no longer be employed. Mr. and Mrs. Cook looked at Mo in disbelief. Through her tears, Mrs. Cook answered, "Merle, you are not going anywhere. You have a job here for as long as you like." Mo's hours picked up, allowing him to work after school, during the summers and at holiday breaks. He walked to work after school and then home to our project on Nunley Street. His walk each day was a distance of about three miles. Later, he worked at Cook's as often as possible as he put himself through the first several quarters of college at Tennessee Tech. Suffice it to say, Granddad Grizzell knew exactly what he was doing.

As time went on, Mo often looked after the rest of us in a "fatherly fashion," as demonstrated when he lectured a young man who drove to our house to pick up Elaine for a date. The young man tooted the horn on his car, rather than step to the door. As any respectable father would do, Mo corrected the young man. In addition, Mo gave me a stern lecture after the way I responded when Gee and I won the third-place prize in the yard contest. Mo was sorely disappointed in me when I jumped to hug the neck of the man who presented me with the twenty-five dollar prize. He quietly explained why my reaction was improper. At sixteen, Mo had become the father figure to all of us. He expected us to be on our best behavior, just as he showed us by his example.

Aunt June, Mother's sister, lived within walking distance of the projects on Nunley Street. She and Uncle Doris lived in a perfect little home which stayed perfectly clean. As you might expect, Uncle Doris got plenty of ribbing about his unusual name. Interestingly, he named his son Doris Junior. Aunt June was an impressive seamstress who ran a lucrative business making custom draperies. Their household had a television and a radio. Of course, we could afford neither. Sometimes, we sat in Aunt June's yard listening to the radio as we drank lemonade, or on Sunday nights, we'd watch *The Ed Sullivan Show* in their living room.

As is common with most girls, I wanted to dress like the women on TV or the older girls at school. I begged and begged until Mother agreed to allow me to wear nylon stockings to school for the first time. Since pantyhose were non-existent, my Aunt June gave me my first garter belt. I was so excited that I went to bed that night wearing my new garter belt and nylon stockings, thinking it would save me time the next morning. Much to my dismay, I woke up with both knees sticking through huge holes in my nylon stockings!

I'm sure Gee and I used that twenty-five-dollar prize money to buy food at the grocery store. Everyday, we would walk the short distance to the store along a dirt road between the project and a cow pasture. We laughed until we cried one day at a poor cow whose hooves were stuck in the mud of the pasture. It's impossible to explain how little it took to make Gee and me laugh. If he looked at me just right, we'd both laughed uncontrollably. We were close friends and although we could fight like animals, we were very protective of each other, much like Mother and her brother. Gee was a quiet child by nature and had very little to say. I always considered my brother to be a "deep thinker." Funny thing about it, to this day, if Gee and I look at each other "eye to eye," we still make each other laugh. We traveled in tandem so often as kids, walking to the store, picking blackberries, playing games, I sometimes wonder if we have subconscious, secret memories that simply cannot be put into words.

{ Sixteen }

GRIZZELL FARM

THE STREET SIGN at the intersection of Grizzell Lane and the Old Smithville Highway provokes numerous happy memories of life with my Grizzell grandparents. Apparently, many in my family feel the same way. Recently, the county had to replace the Grizzell Lane street sign because one of my nephews (who shall remain anonymous) stole it right off the pole.

The Grizzell Farm stretched over several hundred acres in Warren County when I was a young girl. I lived there briefly with my grandparents after we were all evicted from Nunley Street. I was taken to the farm, the boys were at Aunt Dorothy's house and Elaine was with Mommy Hale. Times were really tough and even though the separation was only temporary, we hated to be broken up.

My Granddad had lived on the farm his entire life. What in the world, I often wondered, must it feel like to live in only one house? Later when my grandparents passed away, the farm was sold and transformed into a subdivision. Today, Grizzell Lane is one of the most prominent roads remaining where the farm once thrived. If he were around today, I think Granddad would love to drive his old, black Chevrolet pickup over the roads, now that they have been paved.

For most of his 83 years, my Granddad Grizzell was bigger than life itself. He was a huge man, well over six-feet tall, and very strong and muscular. He was good looking by anyone's standards. I remember Granddad always wearing overalls and using chewing tobacco. His brand was called Sweet Apple. One time when a wasp stung me, Granddad took a big wad of chew from his mouth and put it on the bite to take the sting out. Believe it or not, this made it feel better. I know Grandmother hated that tobacco.

Granddad's full name was Isaac John Grizzell and he was known as "Big Ike." This was partly to distinguish himself from a distant (and smaller) cousin who was called "Little Ike." Granddad was a bright man and for a brief time served as a Tennessee State Representative for Warren and three other counties. When he was asked to cast a vote in exchange for a few dollars, my Granddad knew right then politics was not for him. "If that's the way this is going to work," Granddad said, "then I quit!" The man who took his place, Earnest Crouch, served in the Tennessee legislature for decades. Granddad was also a Justice of the Peace, and for the longest time a portrait of Granddad hung in the state capitol in Nashville. Now, it hangs in the War Memorial Building there.

My Grandmother and Granddad Grizzell had nine children born on the farm. They had three daughters, Faye,

Jane and Dorothy, and six sons, Norman, John Pope, Isaac John, Harold, my father and his twin brother, Lloyd. All six boys served in the armed forces. My grandparents were married for over 60 years and they had 36 grandchildren. As my Grandmother never learned to drive, Granddad took her and the children to Grandmother's church, a Church of Christ, every Sunday. Granddad attended the Methodist church next door where he was a member and played the piano. Grandmother's church did not have any instrumental music, only "a capella" singing. I wonder if Granddad went to his own church just so he could play the piano?

Granddad turned down a football scholarship to attend college in order to stay and work the farm, which he eventually bought from his siblings. The house had six large rooms and tall ceilings. Each bedroom had two big beds and a fireplace. The exterior was white with square columns across the front. The farm had cows, horses and chickens. I remember one of the bulls was named Ol' Red. There was an upper barn near the house and a lower barn across the pasture. The farm had two chicken coops and a smokehouse where the meat was cured. Both structures used to be slave quarters a century earlier, and decades before my family owned the property.

Back then, the men came in from the field for lunch each day at noon and Grandmother always had a hot meal prepared. The men ate first, then the kids and then the women. The granddaughters cleaned up the kitchen. When I was a girl, Granddad would come in for lunch and watch *As The World Turns* on his black-and-white TV set. He would sit in his big, wooden rocker watching what was happening to the Hughes family each week. I promise, sometimes big tears rolled down his cheeks during that soap opera.

Usually, he was a strict and stern person, and downright scary to us kids. That is, until John Chris came along. Before my youngest brother was born, the only other grandchild with red hair was Tim Grizzell. Granddad was partial to Tim, but when John Chris arrived with those big red curls, Granddad turned to mush. John Chris could get away with murder and Granddad always rewarded him with peppermint sticks. Granddad smiled more around that kid than at any other time.

My grandparents' living room, which doubled as their bedroom, had a large fireplace with two big rocking chairs and Grandmother's recliner. It is easy to picture Grandmother, or "Marmie" as my mother called her, sitting in her recliner as she opened her mail every day. She received hoards of cards and letters each week and she was continuously writing notes with well-wishes to sick people. Just like her three daughters, my Aunt Jane, Aunt Dorothy and Aunt Faye, she never missed the birthday of a loved one. I witnessed the number of greeting cards she sent come back to her tenfold. How she loved receiving word from people she cared about. I have observed that some things do not change with time – the impact of a hand-written note is one of those things. Grandmother, like her daughters, was very thoughtful and considerate in that regard.

My grandmother never cut her hair. When she sat upright in a ladderback chair, her hair touched the floor. Washing and brushing it was a long, tedious, time-consuming process. She kept her hair in two long French braids which were meticulously wrapped around her head, then pinned into place. I have many cousins named after my grandmother, Julia Ann Grizzell.

My grandparents slept in a tall, four-poster, cherry bed that was so high, toddlers could literally walk underneath without even ducking their heads. All of their beds had feather mattresses and, to say the least, Grandmother was not very happy when I peed on one at night. She had to beat the mattresses with a broom to facilitate drying them out. Thankfully, I had outgrown bed wetting by the time of this particular stay.

A favorite childhood memory of mine is when the "rolling store" stopped at the Grizzell Farm on scheduled intervals. The store was a large truck about half the size of an eighteen-wheeler. A ramp was pulled from the rear, allowing customers to walk onto the truck which was neatly packed with all sorts of merchandise. Any kind of staple imaginable was stocked in the store, such as sugar, meal, flour, etc. Grandmother sometimes gave us kids three cents each to spend, which was just enough to buy a couple of peanut butter logs, my personal favorite. A nickel would buy an RC Cola and a scoop of Lay's Salted Peanuts. I loved to put the peanuts into the bottle of cola, as I frequently saw my cousins do. The peanuts would sink to the bottom and the beverage became more and more salty as you drank it.

Being one of sixty-three kids who were first cousins provided marvelous, lasting memories; playing together, working together, growing up together. All of the Grizzell cousins pitched in to help on the farm. We had to take turns churning the butter, which was not easy. It was not fun either to walk through the cow poop in the barns to gather eggs, but someone had to do it. I especially loved playing with my cousins Nancy and Penny, who were about the same age as me. Grandmother was strict about many things, but she freely allowed us girls to play "dress up" with her shoes and clothes.

Everyone took their turn helping out. Once, Mo was plowing a potato field with a mule and a one-man plow. But the crazy mule was going too fast and the potatoes were being cut up in the soil, which of course defeated the purpose. Mo gave all the proper commands to make the animal stop, but the mule had a mind of its own. The animal ended up at a big tree and proceeded to start eating the leaves. Well, Granddad had had enough of that mule. I watched as he picked up a 2x4 and slammed it down hard on the animal's head, right between the eyes. Unbelievably, the mule was barely fazed, but it did go back to pulling the plow.

Of course, the Grizzell Farm produced most of the items needed to feed the family. Meat and eggs never had to be purchased. The vegetable gardens and fruit trees gave us many kinds of apples, plums and pears. Grandmother grew huge, tasty muscadine grapes that were wonderful to eat right off the vine. It was like paradise, except for the chickens. I will never forget Grandmother picking up a chicken by the throat and wringing the neck, around and around until it broke. Sometimes, she simply laid the chicken across a big stump and SLAM! Down came the axe and off came the head! Usually, the bird ran around the yard headless for a moment or so. To this day, I am not all that crazy about eating chicken because of those massacres.

Grandmother Grizzell adored my mother. She loved her as if she were her own flesh and blood. In fact, they had a mutual admiration for one another. When I was in the presence of my Grizzell relatives, there was always an unspoken understanding regarding my father. It was obvious he did not provide for us, even though he was perfectly capable. Eventually, he deserted us. When my Granddad Grizzell died the following year, my father was nowhere to be found. The entire Grizzell family was at Granddad's funeral except for my father. My father's brothers and sisters were so unlike him. They loved my father, but they were unhappy about the hardships my mother and my family were forced to endure. Although I knew at a young age there was a strain between my father and his family, the Grizzells always made me feel loved and welcome.

Later, when my Grandmother Grizzell passed away, my mother wrote the following words as tribute to Grandmother:

My mother-in-law possessed so many Christian qualities, it would be impossible to recall them all.

Her name was Julia Ann Sanders Grizzell and I married one of her youngest sons. I went to live at her farm home for a year.

I was a new Christian and a very young seventeen-year old.

I was to learn so many things from my mother-in-law; from gardening and canning to the importance of the Church. She had an indescribably quiet nature and had faith as immovable as a mountain of granite.

I had many times with her alone. During some trying times and problems we had in common, we talked together (and cried together), but many times we laughed together, too. I'm still learning from her and I wish I could tell her that.

My youngest son and I had occasion to be with her often during her last years on this earth. I can picture her in my mind's eye, sitting in her chair with her Bible on a stool by her left side. When the conversation lulled, she read. She truly seemed to have a good relationship with God. Though she left this earth for her place in the better world, her influence lives on.

Ruth Grizzell
Oak Ridge, Tennessee

{ Seventeen }

BONNER STREET

GEE AND I watched from the upstairs window as Mo and his friend destroyed the magazines. The burning pages curled to black and floated though the air in the backyard of our house on Bonner Street. The McMinnville house had three bedrooms; two downstairs and a third upstairs with dormer windows. It had a living room, an eat-in kitchen and a screened porch across the entire back side. I remember the floors throughout were very uneven, especially upstairs, and that the front storm door always slammed shut as it closed. Our yard was large and it backed up to City High School, making it an easy walk for us to attend school.

When we moved in, Mo and his friend found some inappropriate magazines in the attic of our house. Mother found out and insisted the boys destroy them. I will never forget when Gee and I heard them laughing and we ran to the upstairs window to see what was so funny. Mo and his friend were destroying the magazines alright…one page at a time… as they ripped them from the binding and placed them in a small bonfire in the backyard. Of course, they had to examine each page before burning!

Sadly, tragedy would take its toll on us during the year we lived on Bonner Street. Not long after Mo burned the magazines, an emergency vehicle sped its way to our two-story rental house. Mrs. Patton, our next-door neighbor, had phoned for help after hearing Mother's distress call. The ambulance roared down our street with sirens blaring, disturbing the quiet canopy of shady oak trees in this middle-class neighborhood.

A few days prior to his seventh birthday, John Chris developed a severe case of German measles. It was not uncommon for children to experience measles, mumps or chicken pox during that time period. Today, all children are immunized and those diseases are virtually wiped out. We were having a particularly hard time financially. In fact, we were all hungry and John Chris may well have been slightly dehydrated. With no money, no transportation and none of the most basic necessities, Mother had been unable to take my brother to the Warren County Health Department for the second of his two-part MMR inoculation. When John Chris became sick, he was covered in a measles rash and ran a low-grade fever for several days. Mother never left his side, not for a minute.

Doris Whitlock, a wonderful friend from our church, brought enough homemade chicken and dumplings to feed us for a couple of days. My brother began showing signs of improvement when his rash started to fade, however his temperature remained dangerously high for hours at a time.

Mother had been wiping his skin with a cool washcloth which helped to lower his temperature temporarily. Suddenly, my brother's temperature spiked to 106 degrees!

Mother, Gee and I were in the living room with John Chris when his eyes began to glaze over. He became unresponsive when Mother tried to arouse him. Suddenly, his head jerked backward, his arms and legs were rigidly jerking and flailing about. I could see that his jaw was making a grinding motion. He was having a full-blown grand mal seizure! We were terrified, having never seen a seizure before. Mother kept a level head as she prevented John Chris from falling off the sofa or hitting a sharp edge of the furniture. She told Gee to run as fast as he could to the neighbor's house and ask Mrs. Patton to call for help. When the emergency medical technicians arrived, the seizure had passed, but John Chris seemed to be sleeping. They strapped him to a large stretcher which swallowed his small frame and escorted Mother to the front passenger seat of the ambulance. As they sped away, Gee and I stood on the front porch in a stupor, not knowing what was happening or where they were going.

The next thing I remember, Gee and I were looking at our baby brother through a plate glass window in a hospital room. John Chris was surrounded by nurses and doctors as he lay there in a coma. His upper body was covered by a clear oxygen tent. Mother was sitting on a stool next to him with her arms in the tent, holding both of his hands in hers. There were intravenous fluids and anti-convulsive medications infusing into his veins. We learned the dangerously high fever had caused his brain to swell, a condition called encephalitis, and that portions of his brain may have been damaged. I was so worried. Gee was so worried. We all were.

The doctors told my mother the damage may be permanent and irreversible, and that if John Chris ever awoke, there would be more seizures in the future. For many days, Mother sat with my brother as he remained unchanged and unresponsive. She talked to him, sang to him, prayed aloud for him and stroked his arms and legs. Mother was discouraged but determined to see her son come out of his coma. His little mouth was dry from the lack of ingesting fluids, causing his lips to crack. Mother began swabbing his lips with a lemon glycerin-coated cotton swab. All of a sudden, he began slurping up the liquid in the swab, opened his eyes and asked, "Where am I?" John Chris beat all odds, according to the physicians' predictions.

This incident changed everything for our family. John Chris would have to be on two or three medications daily for the rest of his life. Sadly, the medications did not completely control the seizures. They were also very expensive and we had no medical insurance. In addition to striving to keep us fed, clothed and housed, Mother now had to figure out a way to buy the medications. There was no other option, for any time John Chris missed a dose, a seizure was sure to follow. This was a life-or-death situation…and a permanent one.

I will never know how Mother managed to juggle everything alone, but somehow she did. She had an added burden none of us could possibly comprehend. I never once heard Mother complain; she would have done anything for her five children. Many times, she sent Gee and me to the drug store with enough cash to buy medicine for just a day or two. She could not leave John Chris alone for an instant and any monies she made would have to be made from home. She started sewing, crocheting, and mending faster than ever to make extra money.

Everyone chipped in to help however they could. Everyone but my father, that is. Granddaddy Hale gave Mother money and rides to the doctor. My Grizzell grandparents sent vegetables from their garden, plus butter, eggs, cured ham and lard...lots of lard. Elaine was working her job after school making a few dollars a week. With her paycheck, she paid to have a phone put in our house in case we had another emergency. It was the only phone we ever had. Too bad we moved away from this house–that was the end of the phone! After the hospital, it took months to regulate John Chris' medications. He slowly returned to feeling normal, but the rest of us were wrecks. We tip-toed around him terrified of another seizure.

By the time of my baby brother's seizure, I was thirteen years old, I was 5'7" tall and weighed 120 lbs. I looked eighteen. But I was still at that "in-between" stage, when girls are playing with baby dolls one minute and getting into their mother's make-up and high heels the next. I wanted to be all grown up.

Occasionally, Elaine let me go out with her and her friends on Friday nights. In those days, the favorite pastime in

McMinnville was to circle the Dairy Queen, travel a mile up the highway to circle the McDonald's restaurant, and repeat the process over and over. One night, there must have been forty teenagers in a dozen cars and pickup trucks, hanging out. All the cars were "suped up," with big tires and loud mufflers. There was a nineteen-year-old boy who drove a spiffy red car with a black vinyl top. He was a small, squirrely, self-assured guy. He asked my sister if he could take me for a ride in his new car. She thought it would be OK, provided he had me back in a few minutes. My sister would have never agreed, had she known what was in store for me and what he had in mind. She loved me too much for that.

The exact timeline is fuzzy. I am unsure whether the following series of events occurred over a three-, or maybe, a four-day period. I do have vivid memories of what happened... but how long it lasted is unclear. I climbed in the front seat as the car jolted forward, my head flung backwards as he sped away from my sister and her friends. The car was a "4 on the floor," and it climbed to a fast rate of speed in just a few seconds. I was too naïve to realize how dangerous it was to be in a speeding car; in those days, seat belts did not exist. Little did I know, a speeding car was the least of my worries.

We rode to a wooded spot, not far from McMinnville, and he turned off the engine. I recall how dark it was when he turned the car lights off. It was pitch black. We had stopped in a flat, grassy area surrounded by tall trees. When the engine stopped the crickets were singing in unison. The sky was crystal clear and the moonlight was fairly bright. Soon, he reached down to turn the ignition to listen to the radio. The Everly Brothers were singing *All I Have To Do Is Dream*. How could I forget? I thought of that dark night in the woods each time I heard that song in years to come.

He told me he had to get out of the car for a minute. I watched as he walked to the rear of the car. With the addition of the radio came the red brake lights, making it easy to see him lean on the trunk with his back to the window. I was not afraid because it never occurred to me I was in danger. I noticed his elbows going "up and down," and thought maybe he was urinating. This made me embarrassed, so I quickly turned towards the front of the vehicle.

(During my mother's later years, she and I had one conversation about this event. She told me he was probably putting on a condom rather than urinating. At age thirteen, I had never heard of a condom.)

He opened the car door on the passenger side where I was sitting, and motioned for me to scoot over. He was wearing heavy cologne. I think it was Canoe. He leaned toward me, pulling my left knee up and in his direction. I was a pretty strong girl, so I put up as much resistance as I could. Before I could understand what was happening, he had me lying with my back awkwardly stretched over the console. My head and shoulder were sort of wedged under the steering wheel. His weight was causing my back to hurt as I was pressed onto the console. I was fighting to raise my head all the while screaming for him to "GET OFF ME!" He had one hand on my shoulder, and with the other he was reaching up my skirt. I did not understand what was happening, but I knew this was not what I expected; going for a drive is what I expected. I began to cry because the pain was so great. He paused briefly as I was sobbing…then, he forced forward and raped me.

Afterwards, he tried to console me by telling me he loved me. "I want you to wear my senior class ring. We will be going steady." I was drawn up into the fetal position back on the passenger's seat now. We remained in the woods for some time. It was getting very late. When he pulled the car back on the highway, referred to as the bypass, I was relieved to be going back to my sister…only we did not go back to my sister.

The bypass was a long straight road which passed thru acre upon acre of farmland. The rotating red lights of a police car appeared behind us. At that moment, I thought they must be looking for me since we had been gone for more than a "few minutes." The guy punched the gas pedal in an effort to outrun the police. My thirteen-year-old mind never considered the fact that I was a minor and he had crossed a legal line. The car was going SO fast, I could not believe it. Now I was more scared than ever, because I knew if we crashed at this speed I would likely be killed. Pretty soon, the flashing lights faded in the distance behind us. The driver of the car slowed enough to take a right turn off the bypass into a cornfield. The corn stalks were taller than the car. We rode quite a distance into the corn field, stopped the car and waited.

(During the talk I had with Mother years later about that night, I learned in no way had we outrun the police car. The guy in the fast, red car had turned off his lights while we were speeding away from the police. The police officer made the decision to fall back and turn off his flashing lights. The officer was concerned we would have an accident with our car lights turned off, or that oncoming traffic could not see us in the dark. He reasoned it was not worth a chance and that police officer may well have saved my life.)

We were driving, I recall, for what seemed like a long time over mountainous terrain. Most of the roads were not paved. There was no conversation in the car, except the guy was telling me, over and over, it would be alright because we would go steady. He would give me his high school ring and we would go steady. We drove up in front of what looked like a wooden duplex. No people in sight. No cars in sight. If my memory is correct, it was almost daylight. We got out of the car and went inside. I had no idea where we were. All I remember about the inside of the house is the kitchen. The table was metal with a Formica top. The chairs were cushioned covered in clear plastic, like you might see at a restaurant. I sat down at the kitchen table by myself. The guy walked out the door saying something about going to pick up his high school ring. I heard the engine start up with the loud mufflers. I heard gravel being thrown as he drove away. I laid my head in my arms on the table and cried myself to sleep.

I do not know how long I slept. When I woke up, I walked around the kitchen looking out windows, but saw and heard nothing. It was either almost dark again, or a day had passed and the sun was coming up. I was so frightened. I sobbed until there were no tears left and my head was throbbing. My vision was fuzzy with the aura of a migraine headache. I had begun having classic migraine headaches, so I understood why my vision was blurred. There was no telephone in sight. Even if there had been, my family did not have a home phone, and cell phones did not exist. Afraid to go outside, I sat back down at the table. My skirt was damp and I noticed a small puddle on the floor beneath my chair. The only logical explanation was that I must have urinated in my sleep. I was devastated on so many levels. I had been violated, kidnapped, and then left alone in unfamiliar surroundings. Now, I had wet my pants and was in the middle of a fierce migraine headache. What should I do? I needed to think.

Pretty soon, I heard the sound of a smooth engine outside. Clearly, it was not the vehicle which dropped me off; no loud muffler. Terrified because I did not know where I was or who could be outside, I looked for a place to hide. Logically, I should have known my family would find me since they knew who drove me away from my sister. Enough time had passed that the guy was probably back at his home long before now, and he may have been questioned as to my whereabouts.

Suddenly, I heard my Uncle John Leroy's voice calling, "Paula Faye!" I threw open the storm door and ran to his arms. He hugged me and helped me to his car comforting me by saying, "I will take you to your mother now." I only remember Uncle John Leroy, if anyone else was with him, I have no recollection of that.

We were at least ninety miles from home, maybe further. I did not know how my uncle located me in the middle of nowhere. Somehow he found me. He may have saved my life by getting me out of there when he did.

My remembrance of what happened when we arrived back home on Bonner Street was much worse than I anticipated. I knew Mother would grab me and be happy to see me. Never dreaming I would be in trouble, I started getting ready for bed. I crawled into the rollaway bed where I slept with Elaine, so happy to be home. Her boyfriend had recently won several stuffed animals at the county fair, giving me lots of things to cuddle. But then I realized my father was home.

My father stomped into the room barking, "Did you have relations with that boy?" Over and over, I told him no, but he persisted as if I had been a bad girl. He was screaming so loudly that I knew my brothers could hear him. I did not want to disappoint my brothers. Over and over, I denied having relations since I knew my father was going to blame me. Finally, he yelled that he would bring a doctor over to see if I was telling the truth. I cried out, "No, don't get a doctor. It happened! It happened!" My mother always taught us the Bible says we can never hate anyone. Of course, I do not hate my father, but I can say I hate that he demanded we have that conversation in earshot of my brothers. Gee and John Chris did not understand what was happening. Mo set aside a special private time to tell me he loved me and that he believed in me. His words made all the difference in the world. It was typical of Mo to provide emotional support, which he has done my entire life. Even though by this time I had stopped wetting the bed, that night it happened again and I peed all over Elaine; point being, I was still a young girl.

Some period of time passed before I saw the guy with the red car again. It was in a tiny courtroom. Though the room was small, it had beautiful, rich wood floors and wood carvings on the walls and ceiling. I recall two pew-looking benches, divided in the middle making four rows. On one side was me with my parents. On the other side was the guy with his parents. Up in front, there was a wide, tall platform where the judge would sit. Certainly, I had never been in a courtroom before. I guess Mother did not know what to expect and I imagine she had not seen the inside of a courtroom, either.

A police officer told everyone to "rise" because "His Honor" was entering the room. It was Judge Biddle. I recognized the judge because he was a member of the church in Warren County where my family attended services. Mother whispered, "Prayer is a powerful thing." None of the four parents were acknowledged. I was not asked to stand. I was not asked to speak. Judge Biddle called the guy by name, demanding that he walk forward and stand facing him. The question Judge Biddle then asked him are words I would never forget. "Son, you can go to jail for two years or you can join the armed services for two years…your decision. What will it be?" He was off to the army and I never saw him again. Ever.

It was helpful having a large, strong family who

supported me. Somehow, Mother had the wisdom to take the steps necessary to prevent me from carrying "baggage" after this unfortunate chain of events. Certainly, we did not have the means to go to a psychologist or meet with a family counselor. She did three important things for me. First and foremost, she gave me unconditional love and support. Secondly, she made sure I was surrounded by my brothers, uncles and male cousins, who would all be genuinely loving towards me. This showed me the guy who defiled me was the exception, not the rule, and prevented me from mistrusting men in general. Thirdly and most importantly, anyone who is raped heals quicker when they are defended legally. My mother wanted me to know that I was so valuable and important they would never let anyone get away with mistreating me. I understand it would have been easier to sweep it under the rug without ever mentioning it again, which often happens. Instead, Mother did everything in her power to guide me. She often said, "You must hold your shoulders back and be proud of yourself, no matter what your circumstances."

(During the process of completing this writing, I became curious as to whether the kidnap and rape was a part of the permanent record in the county where the incident occurred. Research revealed the records had been expunged. This was disappointing, but not surprising since the father of the culprit was a wealthy business owner.)

I missed a lot of school that year and I had to go to the school clinic many, many times. I was having horrible ocular migraines which caused visual disturbances, making it impossible for me to see the blackboard. My math teacher thought I was faking the migraines because they were so frequent. My schoolwork suffered, to say the least. But Mother was there to help me, encouraging me to keep at it.

That winter, I was a "spot guard" on the school basketball team. Coach Davis was a master at building self-esteem in his team players, which included his daughter who was also named Paula. My teammates displayed undying support in me by making me feel as if the team needed me on the basketball court. I wondered in years to come, whether I was a valuable addition to the team or if their belief in me was what kept me involved? They convinced me that I was irreplaceable. Whatever the reason, the support of my teammates was invaluable. Coach Davis would have forfeited a league title if it meant keeping his students and players even-keeled and well-rounded. I am grateful for his philosophy: that a student's well-being is worth more than wins or championship titles. He may well have just been doing his part at aiding my healing process.

My Christmas memories from Bonner Street are of Mother pacing back and forth on Christmas Eve, looking for my father to come home. He had promised to provide a few dollars for the purpose of buying each of us a gift to unwrap on Christmas morning. The hours were passing with no sign of him. In the wee hours of Christmas morning, there was a knock at the door and a box left on the porch. The box contained a gift for each of us, though they were more like the cheap trinkets you might buy at a truck stop. There was a plastic wallet laced with different colored plastic thread, several tiny plastic cars and a little stuffed chihuahua dog wearing a big-brimmed Mexican hat and a multicolored poncho. We all felt cheapened by our father's gifts, and in some ways, we felt insulted. Recently, one of my brothers brought up this Christmas memory. After all of these years, it still is unforgettable.

Thank goodness my family had my brother Mo to keep us entertained. Mo was now a senior and a model student at City High School. He had a lot of friends and made good grades. Not long before graduation, Mo and a friend decided to pull a school prank which was completely out of character for him. Somehow, he and his friend managed to get their hands on fifteen or twenty old brassieres. One night in the dark, they climbed the only big oak tree in the school courtyard and decorated that tree with the bras like they were ornaments on a Christmas tree! Well, let's just say there was a lot of commotion the next day at school.

The school administrators were furious about the prank and they threatened to cancel the upcoming prom if the guilty party did not come forward. Mo and his buddy did not want to be the cause of their fellow students missing the prom, so they confessed their transgression. Since Mo had never been in trouble before, everyone assumed he was sacrificing himself by telling a lie. The boys were unsuccessful at convincing anyone they had indeed hung the bras on the tree! Mo was told to report to the principal's office the next morning when school was in session. He was mortified to go there for his punishment; not because of the principal, but because the girl he was dating worked in the office. He didn't want Linda, his "dream girl," to witness whatever punishment awaited him. Mo and his buddy were punished for supposedly lying about their confession, but it was never believed they were responsible for this offense.

After an eventful year at Bonner Street, Mother decided to move us back to Oak Ridge. I see now she knew it was in my best interest to have a change of scenery; a new chance. Back then, if a girl was raped, she carried a negative stigma. In fact, one of Mo's senior high classmates asked me for a date. This hurt my brother deeply because he knew what the guy was thinking. By returning to Oak Ridge, Mother was protecting me. It had been eight years since we lived there. And none of us wanted to go.

{ Eighteen }

GEORGIA AVENUE

RETURNING TO OAK Ridge did not make any of us happy. Especially me, since I made the 100-mile trip in the back of an ambulance! At fourteen, I was devastated to be up rooted from McMinnville. My cousins were there, my friends were there, my basketball team was there and my life was there. When it came time to pack our things on Bonner Street, I was bawling like a baby.

We moved out one evening with my father's help. He had borrowed Granddad's truck and loaded it to the brim with our stuff. I was crying so hard as I descended the stairs that I couldn't see, and I tumbled down the steps to the bottom. We had a neighbor call for emergency services as my mother feared I may have had injured my back. To tell the truth, I wonder if I fell on purpose in hopes of preventing us from moving. Off I went to the hospital and everything checked out OK, but the doctor said I should not take a long ride in a car. So, my father arranged for the ambulance service to take me to Oak Ridge, one hundred miles away. Of course, my father never paid for the ambulance. He left the bill for my mother to pay and then disappeared again, this time for months.

Oak Ridge hadn't changed in the decade we were away, and it suddenly felt like we had never left. We moved to a house on Georgia Avenue, which was one of many streets off the Oak Ridge Turnpike named after a state. The streets were in alphabetical order, on one end of the turnpike was Arizona Avenue and on the other end was Wisconsin Avenue. In most cases, the smaller streets which connected with the "state" streets were named after the first letter of the state. For instance, we lived on Viking Road, twice, which ran off Vermont Avenue. Tyrone Street ran off Tennessee Avenue. Meadows Road ran off Michigan Avenue, and so on.

Georgia Avenue was a very nice street with well-kept yards and clean, freshly painted homes. Our house, on the other hand, was the worst house on the street; an absolute dump. Being in high school with new friends, I was so embarrassed to have anyone see where I lived. I would often catch a ride home from school, but then ask to be let out three doors away from our house. I never, under any circumstances, had the opportunity to entertain at our house. Since this was out of the question, my schoolmates didn't need to know exactly where I lived.

The house was dirty and dingy, and the exterior paint was flaking off. I found cans of white paint in the crawl space, so I painted the outside of that house all by myself. I think I painted some of the windows, too. It was obvious I was not proficient at house painting, especially since the paint I found was *interior* paint, but I had to do something to spruce it up. I remember that I painted only three sides of the house because one side was not visible from the road. I didn't paint the porch, which was fairly large. Maybe, I ran out of paint.

It was a "B" house with two bedrooms and, as usual, this meant Mother did not have her own room. I didn't always know where she slept, but in this particular house my mother had a cot tucked away in the kitchen. She was always awake when we went to sleep and she was always awake when we got up. I'm certain she did not want to call attention to the fact that she did not have a bed of her own. My mother was humble and so determined, the last thing she would do was have us hear her complain. Today, we worry about making sure the sheet sets on our beds are perfectly matched; my mother didn't have a bed of her own, let alone perfectly matched sheets. She had no chest of drawers for her clothes. Few as they were, she kept them in a laundry basket. And through all of this, she never, ever complained.

I remember being really hungry at the house on Georgia Avenue and that sometimes we had no electricity. As with other places we lived in Oak Ridge, we were close enough that we could walk to the store. Gee and I usually walked just about every single day to get bread, milk, or some staple that Mother needed to keep us fed. I remember Gee's birthday that year. Mother made a huge skillet full of fried potatoes for his birthday treat. Potatoes were cheap and easy to store, so we had them with most meals. Mother had a knack for making wonderful treats with whatever we had in the cupboard. We had snow ice cream at least once every winter. Her fudge recipe is the best I have ever had. Some of us liked peanut butter fudge, which she would add during times when we could afford it. If Mother could manage to have us in our own beds at night, warm and fed, then that was all that really mattered to her. Her unselfishness was immeasurable.

She remained hard working as a seamstress and worked from home in order to care for John Chris properly. She crocheted baby booties, baby sweaters and baby caps for different people who placed private orders. She made them for whoever wanted them and charged a nominal fee of $5 to $10, which was enough to see that her children were fed. My mother's hands were never idle, her thimble was always on her finger.

While we lived on Georgia Avenue, Mother scraped up enough money to purchase a used sewing machine. She hadn't had one in a while and this really helped her as she provided for us in terms of clothing. I can honestly say, I do not ever remember Mother buying any of us a store-bought outfit. Mo bought us clothes after he started his job, and our aunts and uncles would sometimes buy things for us, especially shoes. But, I do not ever remember walking into a store with my mother to buy clothes. It was simply unheard of. Often, she would buy used draperies or curtains at a junk sale and turn them into beautiful blouses or skirts for me and my sister, but rarely for herself. She was constantly doing for others and those in need.

Mother made Gee a shirt that year, and at that time, many of the young men were wearing fashionable cotton madris shirts with a loop in the back. The loop designated the brand, or the designer who made the shirt. For his birthday, Mother had hand-made a beautiful pin-point oxford cotton shirt for Gee, and somehow managed to make a loop and put in on the back. It looked like a shirt you would see in a fashion magazine. Gee was dashing in that shirt.

Ever since we moved from McMinnville, I had missed my friends. Of course, we did not have a phone, so we had to borrow one from the neighbors. In those days, to pay for a long-distance call you simply told the operator your name and phone number. When I called McMinnville, I'd give a bogus home number so I wasn't charged for the call. A few months later, the phone company caught on and a representative came to our house to give me a stern warning. I was busted. But hey, I missed my friends! At fourteen, I guess I was starting to look for ways to beat the system. My mother made it crystal clear to me that giving a bogus phone number was dishonest.

It seems we lived on Georgia Avenue for three or four months at the most. One day, a man in a dark suit knocked on the door and told us we had twenty-four hours to vacate the property. My poor little mother; the look on her face broke my heart. Where were we going to go this time? Having no phone made it pretty hard to search for a house or apartment, having no automobile made it impossible to move about.

My mother had some special friends who watched out for us. Dora Forest and Ann Nygard were ladies who had been close to Mother since before I was born. Mother was quickly becoming best friends with Nezzie Allen, who helped us any way she could. Nezzie located our next rental house and loaned Mother the money for the down payment. We packed as much as we could in Nezzie's car and off we went.

{ Nineteen }

QUINCY AVENUE, 1968

BY NOW, THE pattern had been firmly established. Mother would find enough money for one or two months rent, and then hope and pray that our luck would change for the better. Mother took it day by day. She continued to believe my father might wander in at any time to help out. Or, she believed that our landlord would find it in his or her heart to give us more time. Time we had, but money we did not. After three or four months would pass, we would inevitably be asked to leave. Mother would find a new rental and the pattern would start all over again. Through it all, we saw our mother striving to make the best of each tough situation, "rising above" whatever circumstance we found ourselves in.

We all thought we hit pay dirt when Mother and Nezzie drove us to our new house. Holy cow! It was the same Quincy Avenue house we lived in when I was two years old. It was a great house; a small, framed, three bedroom with a huge yard. It was clean and freshly painted. It was beautiful and exactly the same as we remembered it. The babbling brook was still out back. It's funny that we had some of the same neighbors from the first time we lived there over a decade earlier.

Once we moved in, the house seemed so spacious. But we realized later, this was because some of our furniture was lost in the process of moving. When you are evicted and a lock is put on the door, you can't exactly go back for more of your belongings. The house on Quincy was a little further distance to the grocery store and to school, so Mother arranged for rides from neighbors, friends and people from church. She always arranged for someone to pick us up for church. Even if Mother could not go for some reason, she saw to it that her children did.

Mother instilled her work ethic in each of us by making us get jobs early in life. When at Quincy Avenue, I landed my first job! I became gainfully employment at Western Auto, a chain appliance store in Oak Ridge. It was located in the only shopping center in town and, fortunately, the store manager allowed me to work as many hours as I could be present. I earned an impressive $2.30 per hour. Initially, my responsibility was to convince customers to open a Western Auto charge account. I stood behind a plain card table on the sidewalk outside the store, which was always busy with shoppers. Every day, I stood there with my charge card applications in hand, finding the words to convince passers-by to open an account.

The manager was very happy with my performance, so he promoted me to the cash register inside and to help out on the sales floor. I worked there during summers, holidays and weekends throughout high school. My first employment opportunity was a life saver. I learned through osmosis how to help the customers locate the items they were searching for and if I did my job well, convince them to buy a few additional items, too.

Not having a telephone of our own made it nearly impossible to keep up with my new friends. As a teenage girl, I wanted to be like everyone else. I wanted nice clothes, I wanted a car for my family and I really, really wanted a phone. I wanted it all. Regrettably, I spent very little time in consideration of what Mother was enduring. As a matter of fact, if you wanted to get on Mother's bad side, all you had to do was start complaining about how hard life was, or perhaps complain that the electricity was off for days at a time. She would quickly remind you about the good things we had in our lives, such as being together and being healthy. With the exception of John Chris' seizure disorder and my recurring trips to the hospital, all five of us kids enjoyed wonderful health. Mother was good at making sure we appreciated those things, rather than concentrating on what we did not have.

The Oak Ridge community swimming pool always made for heated discussions. I used to love to hang out at the pool, which was considered one of the largest spring-fed public pools in the nation. Mother did not like it when I went there, so if I managed to go, it was usually because I "snuck." Mother would have never approved of what I wanted to wear as a teenage girl. Although looking back, I seriously doubt that I got away with anything. Our mother had eyes in the back of her head. I believe she saw and heard everything when it came to her children. I remember one summer day, I knew my friends were going to congregate at the pool and I was really begging hard for Mother to let me go. I had been to the pool the day before and I'm sure my mother knew that. "You need to stay home today, Paula Faye," Mother said. I remember Linda, Mo's girlfriend, looking at me out of the corner of her eye. "Paula, you should do what your mother says the first time she says it," Linda told me directly, "and you should not continue to beg her as you are." I did not want to disappoint Linda, for I had a lot of respect for her.

I adored my mother, but I gave her a really hard time. I was a stubborn teenager and strong-willed almost to a fault. Although I respected Mother tremendously, I sassed her and rolled my eyes if I did not like the answers she gave me. My siblings were model children, especially Gee. As a boy, Gee was shy, sensitive and easily embarrassed. He was an extra good kid and never caused Mother any trouble. Gee never "snuck" anywhere. He always obeyed the rules and he never sassed. But not me. One day, I had mouthed-off about one thing or another and Mother turned to get her switch. Elaine was there that day and we looked at each other as Mother headed towards me. So, we got on each side of Mother and picked her up by her elbows. Now, both Elaine and I are 5' 7" and Mother was all of 5' 2," so we lifted Mother up high enough that her feet were off the ground. "You put me down!" she said laughing as we tickled her. All three of us laughed very hard.

We were all growing up. The last time we lived at Quincy Avenue, we were just little kids. John Chris hadn't even been born yet. Now, Elaine was 22 and Mo was 20. Elaine was the most unhappy of all of us when our family moved back to Oak Ridge. Like me, she hated to be uprooted from her friends.

Soon after we came back to Oak Ridge, Elaine married her grade-school sweetheart. Mother made Elaine's wedding gown, her own dress and my dress, too. She made all of these by hand and they fit each of us perfectly. Elaine's dress was simple but elegant. Mother found the white satin on a garment remnant rack. The dress had short sleeves and a fitted waste with a long, full skirt. Elaine wore white house slippers underneath, but you could not tell because of the floor-length skirt. Mother's dress was a pink shirt-waste dress. My dress was a baby blue shift with a bow for my hair made from the same fabric. It was pretty and feminine. I wanted so badly to wear makeup with this dress, but Mother and I did not agree. After much pleading, she prevailed, though she allowed me to wear mascara. There were no flowers at the wedding and the ladies at the church made an array of desserts for a little reception afterwards. Mother made a tiered wedding cake. Mo bought a suit for Gee, John Chris and himself at J.C.Penney's. It was the first suit Gee and John Chris ever wore. Our father was there to walk Elaine down the aisle, paid nothing towards the wedding and then went missing in action. Coincidently, soon after Elaine and her husband were married, they moved into the same apartment on Viking Road where our family had lived in 1958. Talk about déjà vu!

Elaine and her husband had three beautiful, blonde,

blue-eyed children. In her adult life, my sister had a profitable, professional career working for the Environmental Protection Agency. Lately, she has been struggling with her health, but I believe my sister would tell you the best thing that ever happened to her was the recent addition of several adorable grandchildren. She enjoys them every day.

After high school, Mo stayed near McMinnville and attended Tennessee Tech. His girlfriend from high school, Linda, went to nursing school in Nashville. Though he hoped it wouldn't happen, Mo was drafted into the armed services while at college. The war in Vietnam was escalating year after year, and by now it was in the news every day. Mo joined the navy, married Linda and then said a very tearful goodbye the day he left for the service. I remember clearly what an awful day that was. However, once the navy found out Mo was married, they didn't want him. So, Mo and Linda moved to Oak Ridge and they ended up finishing college in nearby Knoxville. Deep in his heart, Mo knew the navy was not where he was supposed to be. One clear sign of this was on the draft notice itself, where his name, Merle, was misspelled as Mule!

My eldest brother, always the model student, worked his way through college and he and Linda have two children. Mo is a very humble person and someone who has been successful in every walk of life. He raised his family in Florida before he became a Human-Resource Director in Chicago with Sears. My brother always planned to return to his Tennessee roots and after a management career with Sears, he came home to live outside of Nashville. Today, Mo spends much of his time working with Eastern European Missions and is very passionate about putting Bibles and spiritual materials into the hands of school children in eastern Europe and Russia. He is a wonderful brother, husband, father and a doting grandfather.

Memories of our stay on Quincy Avenue in 1968 are few since we lived there less than three months. I was sad to move from this nice house, especially since we had so many fond memories during our first stay there. Sometimes, I like to look at the photograph of our family standing outside the house when we were just little kids. The photo was probably taken in 1957, or so. A tricycle sits on the sidewalk. Two little children's chairs sit on the front porch. Laundry hangs from a clothesline out back. If ever we had a house that was our home, this was it.

Me in 6th grade in McMinnville after I had a tooth pulled.

West End Avenue: Mother, me and Elaine.

West End Avenue: from left, Uncle Tim, Mo and Gee.

Playing "dress up" with Uncle Clark's niece, Bernice, at Aunt Faye's house.

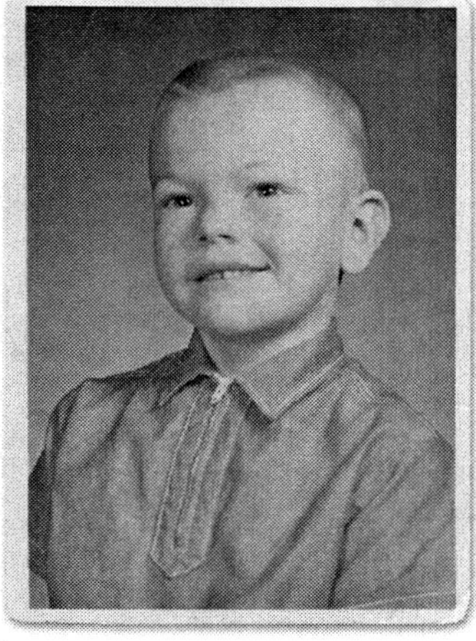

Grade school pictures in McMinnville. Me in 7th grade, left, and my brother, John Chris, in 2nd grade. John is wearing a shirt that Mother made.

My grandparents, Granddaddy and Mommy Hale.

Uncle Tim, Mother's youngest brother, heading to Vietnam

Granddad Grizzell with my cousin Kenneth and John Chris.

Grandmother Grizzell sitting in her recliner and writing a letter.

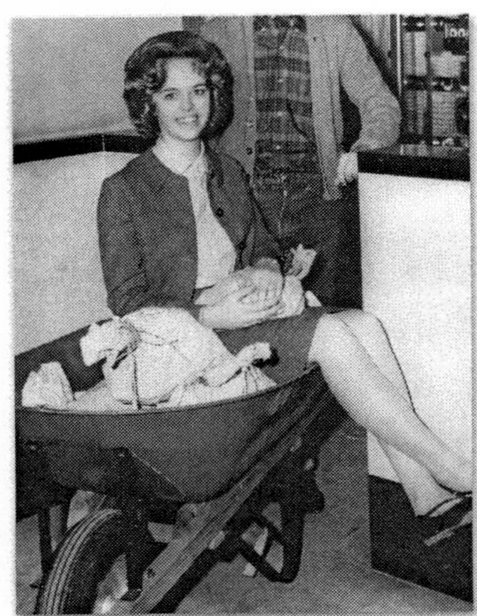

Elaine pictured as "most likely to succeed" in her senior yearbook in McMinnville.

Mo and Linda the year they graduated from high school in McMinnville.

Elaine's wedding, from left, Gee, Elaine (in her house coat), John Chris, my father, Mother, me and Mo.

Photo booth snapshot of John Chris and Mother's first grandchild, Greg.

Me as a junior at Oak Ridge High with bleached hair.

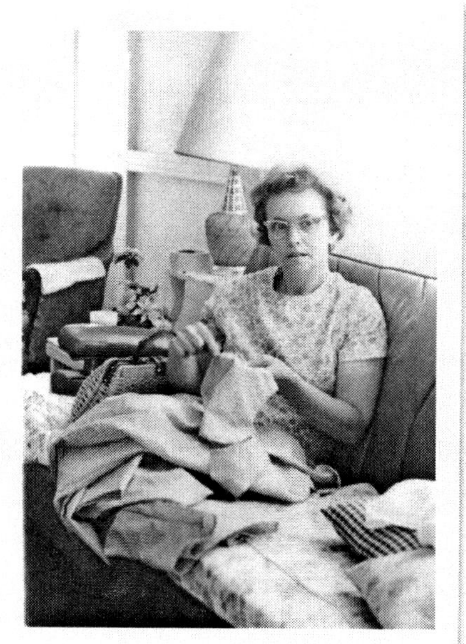

Mother, the way I remember her most: sewing with a pile of fabric on her lap.

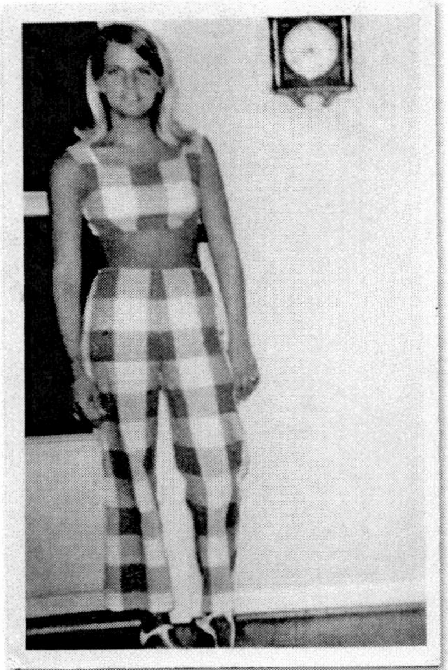

Pelham Road: me wearing an outfit Mother made, how she hated the way I wore it!

Groovy! That's me, second from right, in a local fashion show. My friend, Donna Pitt, is at right.

Me as a senior at Oak Ridge High.

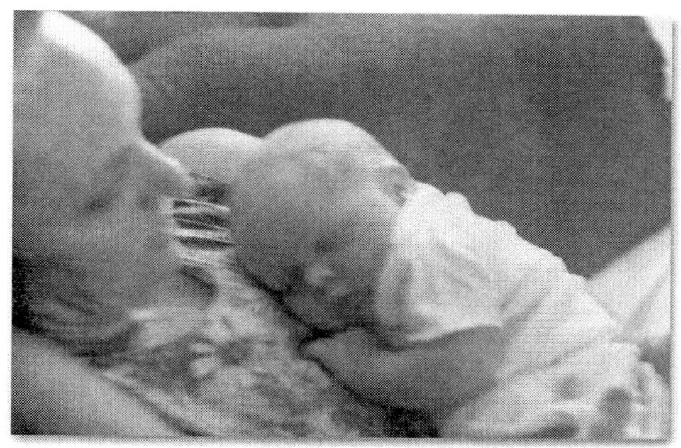

Mother with her grandson, Doug.

John Chris, going to play the drums at a school concert.

Mother and Gee in his tuxedo.

A beautiful picture of Mother and her granddaughter Amy.

Mother, in front, with the five of us. From left, Mo, me, John Chris, Elaine and Gee.

Mother, center, adored her younger sisters: June, left, and Jane Ann.

Mother, right, and Nezzie Allen, a few months before Mother passed away.

{ Twenty }

PARSONS ROAD

"SHHH...BE QUIET! Someone is trying to break into the house" are the words my father whispered deep in the night at Parsons Road. I was scared out of my wits. Gee and John Chris were in their bunk beds, I was on the old rollaway bed that Elaine had bequeathed to me. Everyone was frozen with fear. There was loud clamoring and banging at the front door and the back door at the same time. Who were they and what did they want?

It did not occur to me that intruders would not make such loud banging noises in the middle of the night. After what seemed like forever, the knocking stopped and the men left. When daylight came, my father slipped out the back door without making a sound. Later, we learned that it was the police at our door. They had tracked my father to our house looking to make an arrest. My father had been writing bad checks, causing many of his vendors to go unpaid. The vendors had every right to recoup their money and request that a warrant be issued for my father's arrest. Of course, Mother had no money and could not help him. So, the only thing left for my father to do was to disappear at first light, something he was pretty good at already.

I often thought about my father. When we moved without notice, I wondered how he would find us? I felt sure he wanted to see his family. But where was he sleeping? By this time, Mother was already hearing rumors which she did not share with us. She did a wonderful job protecting us from all of the "bad stuff."

Our place on Parsons Road was a dilapidated, "flat-top" style house. It was a one-bedroom structure that was square in shape with a flat roof. The house sat on a foundation of brick piers and in some spots the siding was falling off. It was located in Oak Ridge in a desirable neighborhood called Woodland. As usual, our house stuck out as the most run-down structure on this pristine street. I think my family lived at this house for a very short period. Elaine and Mo were married, so Gee, John Chris and I were the only kids left at home.

John Chris was now ten years old and it had been a several years since his encephalitis. We all adored our brother. We hauled him around and played with him a lot. Mother was very protective of John Chris when he was still this young. She had few shortcomings, but one of them was how much she blamed herself for my brother's epilepsy. She felt it was her "failure" for not getting us all properly inoculated. She spent an inordinate amount of time caring for John Chris, but never once made him feel like a burden. I will never know how she managed to provide him with the anti-convulsive medications that were vital to his survival. For us, health insurance was an unheard of luxury. Mother taught us the importance of how to react should John Chris have a seizure. Usually, the plan was for one of us to run as fast as we could to a neighbor's house and ask someone to call emergency services. We knew to remove sharp or otherwise dangerous objects. John Chris had a cluster of small seizures one day. I remember paramedics came to our house but they didn't take him to the hospital. By the time they got there, the seizures had subsided. They checked John Chris out, then spent time explaining to Mother this was going to be a normal part of his condition. And so, life went on.

I continued working at Western Auto where I was given more and more responsibility. When the Christmas holiday season rolled around, I genuinely enjoyed being at work. The store and the shopping center were draped in multicolored lights which were so festive. Everyone was in a good mood. Christmas carols were played in the store, but not loud enough to drown out the "ding" of the bell which rang each time a customer entered the front door. I was one of five or six sales clerks working during the holiday. Each of us followed a customer through their merchandise selections, rang-up the sale and offered to gift wrap the items.

The store was really busy with customers one day before Christmas, and I was gift-wrapping item after item. I would wrap a toaster for a customer and then, without thinking, I'd take a battery-operated hair dryer off the shelf and gift wrap it for Elaine. Next, it was a battery-operated shaver for Mo, and then remote-control race cars for Gee and John Chris. What was happening? I was wrapping nice presents for each of my family members without paying for them. Why was I stealing from Western Auto?

This was a terrible thing to which I never confessed. I do not know what came over me, but I wrapped one gift after another for my family. At the end of my shift, I had a load of gift-wrapped boxes. My manager trusted me, never dreaming I had not paid for the merchandise. Certainly, I knew better. I stole toasters, waffle irons, crock pots and tools galore. All of a sudden, every gadget imaginable at Western Auto was within my grasp. I do not remember stealing anything for myself, although I probably did.

My conscience was killing me and I knew I had committed an awful offense. Deep down, I was miserable knowing I had forfeited my honesty to provide these useful items to my family. After years of having so little, I traded my clean conscience for an abundant Christmas. I thought back to when I was a little girl at the May Day celebration at grammar school. I thought about the little rag doll I stole from the drug store that day, and how mad my mother was at what I had done. Guilt is an awful feeling and I am still sorry to this day.

{ Twenty One }

LABORATORY ROAD

DURING MY JUNIOR year in high school, the family moved to an old, abandoned warehouse on Laboratory Road in Oak Ridge. The warehouse was sandwiched in a row of industrial buildings near the atomic energy plant. It was Mother, Gee, John Chris and myself. My father dumped us there and drove away. The building was huge with just one large room. It looked to be about the size of a football field. There were several big barrels scattered here and there, along with bits of trash. I clearly remember my father borrowing a truck from a man named Jack in order to move our things. There was very little to move since we lost more and more of our personal items each time we relocated. I think we stayed on Laboratory Road for only three to four days.

"Well now, this will be kind of like an experiment," Mother said looking at the warehouse. She always worked very hard to keep us from the cold realities of our situation, but this time, it was impossible to hide the facts. My father had dropped us off at an abandoned warehouse with no food or transportation. There was no electricity, no bathroom and no running water. I distinctly remember Mother keeping us out of school during this time. She kept all of our report cards and I have all of mine to this day. The number of tardy and absent days is astounding, although I know she did the very best she could to keep us in school. The only time my report card showed perfect attendance was the year I lived with my Aunt Faye in Murfreesboro.

My mother had many loyal friends in Oak Ridge who seemed to drop in at the most opportune times. I recall Ann Nygard and Dora Forrest bringing hot meals while we were there. Ann had four children and often took us to her house for hours at a time to play and, more importantly, to eat. The few nights we slept in the warehouse, we slept side-by-side on the floor on a blanket. Thankfully, it was not cold outside, so Mother did not have to worry about keeping us warm. Mother provided us the important kind of warmth. Warmth of her loving arms and the smile which assured us everything would be all right. Her angelic smile was decorated with great dimples! Mo and Gee were lucky enough to inherit her dimples.

One day, two men arrived at the warehouse. One man identified himself as Jack, the person who my father had borrowed the truck from. Jack told us my father had not returned with his truck and he was asking if we knew where it was. We didn't have a clue. The third or fourth day, someone began banging on the metal door at just about nightfall. He was a tall, muscular man in a navy-colored uniform and he said he was a deputy sheriff. He told my mother it was unlawful for us to stay in the building which was government property. It was unsafe and it did not have water for drinking or bathing. Just as he was offering to take us to a shelter, Dora Forrest drove up and rescued us. She took Mother, Gee, John Chris and myself to her house. All four of us slept in Dora's living room on a fold-out sofa. Somehow, Mother managed to make it seem like this was all part of "our experiment," so we would not feel so embarrassed.

Dora was a dear, dear friend, who kept a close eye on our needs. She made the best coconut pie in the world. She helped Mother obtain food stamps, which was a life saver. We were evicted from several homes growing up, but the night the sheriff's deputy made us move was one of the worst nights of my life.

{ Twenty Two }

ELZA GATE

ELZA GATE WAS a community a few miles east of Oak Ridge. A few miles is a long way for a family who has no transportation. Mother, Gee, John Chris and I were stuck there for a few months. The house was on a very busy highway. It was a nice house with a fireplace in the main room, and it was virtually empty, except for our clothes. Our voices echoed as the sound bounced off the hardwood floors. There were no curtains on the windows, other than the sheets Mother tacked up as a means of gaining privacy. I cannot remember how we physically got to the house at Elza Gate. After we were evicted from the abandoned warehouse, we stayed with Dora Forrest for a few days. It is difficult to imagine how any landlord allowed us to rent a house. Of the twenty-five places I lived prior to turning eighteen, we lived in eighteen of those places in twelve years.

Under other circumstances, Elza Gate would have been a lovely place to live. We were just across the highway from the beautiful, broad Clinch River. Other families who lived on the river enjoyed boating, swimming, water skiing or fishing. We were busy trying to survive. The only other house nearby was quite a distance down the road and around a sharp curve. The nights were very dark. Since we were far enough away from Oak Ridge, there were no street lights. Even though we had lived in the country many times before, I considered myself a city girl. Living out in the middle of nowhere was miserable. Elza Gate was too far away for me to see my friends or to go to work at Western Auto. Mother, Gee, John Chris and I would go days without seeing another human being, except when Gee and I made our jaunts to the store.

I honestly believe Gee and I walked to the grocery store every single day we lived in that house. We would walk across the busy road to a graveled lane, which led to the back of the store where the boaters gassed their rigs. It was embarrassing to go into the store to sell our Coke bottles in hopes of buying a loaf of bread, or a gallon of milk. Back then, it was common for people to throw litter out automobile windows, especially soda bottles. Gee and I spent many hours scanning the side of the road, collecting bottles which sold for three cents each, if my memory serves me. It seemed that each day we had just enough to buy whatever necessities were most important.

The most prominent memory of living at Elza Gate makes me shiver to this day! There was a huge, black snake which terrorized me. That snake lived in the front yard, very close to the front porch. He was six feet long if he was an inch…which is not an exaggeration! The snake would lay across the grass with his head held high, just daring Gee and I to step out on the porch. When we had to go out, we ran out the back door trying to fool that old snake. That reptile clearly controlled me. I cannot speak for Gee, but I believe he was as afraid as I was.

Somehow, one of my brothers managed to sneak a rabbit into the house. The only pet we ever had was Monkeyface, the cat who fled when I was around six years old, so having a pet rabbit was quite unusual. Mother reasoned she already had enough trouble feeding us without adding a hungry rabbit to the mix. Not to worry, the rabbit ate everything in sight. He ate the leather straps off our burlap firewood carrier. He ate our belts, our shoelaces and the soles of our shoes. Anyway, I was afraid of that stupid rabbit, too. I don't know why I did not feed him to the snake!

After moving back to Oak Ridge, Mother was pleased to be reunited with an old friend from her past. Agnes Hogg and her family went to church with us when we were little. She and Mother got along famously because they were both such crafty people. Agnes was an accomplished painter and seamstress. She heard we had moved to Elza Gate and was kind enough to drop in one day. It's not like anyone could call ahead, so Agnes came over with baked goods…and an entrepreneurial proposition. Agnes had begun producing a teeny porcelain doll with a cloth body and a sculptured face, hands and feet. The doll was called Sugar Lump and she needed someone to crochet clothes for the dolls. So, she thought of Mother. They quickly went to work and sold several of their first dolls right away. The Sugar Lump factory was up and running!

When my brothers and I were cleaning out Mother's house after she passed away in 2008, we came across several of her Sugar Lump dolls. We also came across a diary. It had a red cover and a cloth strap which wrapped around the outside of the book to fasten it shut. The strap was torn and broken and the pages inside had yellowed. The binding was falling apart and many of the pages were hanging on by only a thread. But it was the most beautiful thing I had ever seen, for the diary belonged to Mother. Who knew she kept a diary? I now held in my hands a day-by-day account of my mother's life during the last few years that I lived at home. Page after page, her writing was quite clear. How I can recognize her handwriting anywhere! Remarkably, she added entries almost daily.

She wrote about everyday events…
—*John Chris and I got a cab and went to church. Elaine came and got us and brought us home.*

She wrote about her health…
—*I have been sick all day. Not able to sit up all day.*

She wrote about finances…
—*Ann Nygard came over. We went downtown. She took me to get food stamps.*

—*I got a check in the mail today for $90 from the welfare department for the month.*

But mostly, she wrote about my father, Floyd...

—*I had a letter from Floyd. He wants to see me. I do not know why. He claims he has filed for bankruptcy.*

—*Today, Floyd is 45 years old. We do not know where he is.*

—*This is Saturday. Floyd did not come home as usual.*

—*All the children were here for Xmas. Some boy came here and brought John Chris a mandolin from Floyd and a note on a sheet of notebook paper saying "Merry Xmas."*

I cherish her diary as I do her thimble. I cried the first time I read it. When I read it again, I realized Mother confided all of her worries and heartaches in this little red book, rather than complain to her children.

{ Twenty Three }

PELHAM ROAD

THE KIDS I ran around with at Oak Ridge High were the track, football and basketball athletes of the school. Generally, they were a very clean-cut group. During that time, girls were not allowed to play sports after the ninth grade, so for me, my basketball days were over. However, I would go to many of the school meets, games and matches with my friends, as long as I could afford the $1 admission. A popular spot to go on Friday nights was the Armory, which was a clean, wholesome place to congregate. Everyone loved to go to the Armory for school dances. Per Mother, going to dances was not allowed, so I snuck there several times. Everybody else went to the Armory on Friday nights, so I thought I should, too.

Mother let me "group date" when I turned sixteen. A bunch of boys and girls would all go together for an evening out. Usually, we went to Carbide Park, a grassy area beside a small lake near one of the atomic energy plants, or we'd spend time at the roller skating rink or the bowling alley. When I was a junior, I bleached my hair with lemon juice in a homemade concoction. I have a snapshot of myself with my bleached hair and wearing an orange and white checked top and pants, which Mother made from a sheet. Mother and I had a huge problem over this outfit because I would tuck my top under my bra, making it a midriff top. Mother just about died that I was showing my midriff, but I loved that outfit!

The juniors and seniors at Oak Ridge High School enjoyed good clean fun. I did not know of anyone who drank alcohol or smoked pot; marijuana was barely on the scene in Oak Ridge in the late sixties. Many of the kids smoked cigarettes, but I did not. Oak Ridge is very wooded and some of the boys at school cleared out a large space on a ridge behind one of the plants. To access the area, you had to follow an obscure, make-shift path through deep woods. The boys named our secret place The Circle, and only a few select kids knew about it, including me. At night, we would build a fire and watch the sparks fly up into the darkness. We'd sit on a blanket, talk, sing and look at the stars. When we didn't have a fire, The Circle became pitch black when we turned off our flashlights. When we were there, we felt miles away from the rest of the world. I wonder if anyone else remembers it like I do?

My best friend in high school was Donna Pitt, who was the head majorette in our school marching band. Donna was bright and beautiful, a poised and talented dancer. She entered and won several beauty contests. Donna was often asked to model in a variety of fashion shows. A few times, she arranged for me to model in small group events with her. I had no formal training and was anything but poised, so Donna taught me how to pose for the pictures. In fact, she and her mom, Gladys, introduced me to a number of cultural events. Donna and her mom lived just around the corner from us the brief time we were on Pelham Road. Donna frequently picked me up for school functions and social events in her gold Pontiac. At that time, gasoline was twenty-seven cents a gallon. We'd scrape together enough money for two or three gallons, which was just fine to get around town. I was about as unsophisticated as a person could be under the circumstances. The only movie I had ever seen was *The Sound of Music*. When Donna invited me to watch *Romeo and Juliet* at the movie theater at Jackson Square, she was shocked to learn I did not know the storyline. I cried like a baby when Romeo and Juliet died.

I will never forget the sad day when I was hanging out at Donna's house and an emergency phone call was received. Her father, who piloted his own private airplane, had been killed in a tragic crash. My heart broke for Gladys, Donna and her brother Ronnie. I waited there with Donna until her mom could get home to her. Donna was so traumatized, I remember wishing I could "fix it" for her.

Another memorable visit at Donna's house resulted in a trip to the emergency room at Oak Ridge Hospital. I developed severe and unexplained abdominal pains one day. After a few hours, the pain worsened and Gladys was concerned that I may have had appendicitis. She knew it would be a help to Mother if she took matters into her own hands and sought medical advice on my behalf. At the hospital, Donna and Gladys were kind enough to stay in the room when the doctor was there. While it was reasonable for the ER physician to perform an internal examination, it was unreasonable for him to make judgmental comments and accusations. In a harsh and gruff voice he spoke, "Are you pregnant? Because, you are not a virgin!" I was not pregnant, but of course, I was not a virgin. I had never shared the story of my kidnap and rape with Donna or anyone, but now it was necessary to do so. Subconsciously, I thought not talking about it would help me forget about that awful experience. I thought forgetting about it would unbreak my heart.

Even though I told Donna, I could never muster up the courage to confess to my other friends that I had been attacked. The kids at The Circle were very close knit and we swore to share everything about ourselves, but there, in the glow of the campfire in the dark woods, I could never find the right words. I was afraid my friends would not think well of me. Girls who had been molested were labeled in a very unfavorable way. It took me several decades to "rise above," as Mother so ably taught us to do.

Donna Pitt and I lost touch after graduation, but we were reunited at our twentieth high school reunion. What a blast it was to see her! She is part owner in a dance studio which works with champion dance teams. At one time, she was one of the choreographers for the Dallas Cowboys Cheerleaders. Her friendship is very dear to me.

Sadly, my family's stay at the house on Pelham Road was so short lived, we never completely unpacked our belongings. The spacious three-bedroom house was in a beautiful neighborhood in Oak Ridge. This was one of the nicest houses we ever lived in. We must have paid the first month's rent only because we moved after about five or six weeks. Clearly, the owner of the property was not interested in allowing us to live there rent free. Mother was especially tense while we lived on Pelham Road. She obviously knew we would be on the run very soon. Mother's friend, Nezzie Allen, was there to help however she could and she was quickly becoming one of the family. Mother was worried sick about John Chris and his medication, where we would live next, and quite frankly, what we would eat from day to day. Bless her heart, I think the stress made her crochet all that much faster.

—*We are in trouble about the rent. I talked to collection agency. She says we have to be moved by Monday or pay $635.*

—*I took some crocheted booties to Kramer's and Sterns today. They took them on consignment.*

—*We got a notice to move and a light bill for $105.*

However, Mother did have something wonderful to smile about during this time. Actually, two reasons to smile. Mo and Elaine each had a baby son a few months apart; one was blonde and blue eyed, the other had brown hair with brown eyes. Mother crocheted each a baby sweater with matching caps and booties. She now had two beautiful grandsons that she loved more than life itself. "There is nothing like a little boy," I heard her say.

{ Twenty Four }

PURDUE AVENUE

WE HAD MIGRATED back to a government project during my senior year, hoping the rent would be more affordable there. The apartment on Purdue Avenue in Oak Ridge was a two-story, two-bedroom, brick dwelling. I remember the floors were white-speckled tile with layers of floor wax, making them very slick. John Chris loved to slide across the floor in his socked feet.

The first night we moved in, Mother made fudge. She asked me to unpack the few boxes which came with the move so she would have time to dedicate to sewing. She was making dresses for Ann Nygard's daughters, Cathy and Pam. Ann was a seamstress as well, and a good friend. She may have asked Mother for the clothing in order to help us financially. From the projects on Purdue, I could easily walk to work at Western Auto. I worked as much as I could after school and on Saturdays. In those days, most shops were closed on Sundays. No one ever found out about the Christmas when I gift-wrapped presents for my family. And I never said a word.

My father was around during this time. To all of us, it

was no big deal when he arrived. We were used to his coming and going. Mother was increasingly frustrated with my father's behavior. It was so unfair for her. When he was away, he always managed to stay one step out of touch. She never knew exactly where he was or when he was coming home next.

—Floyd away all day. Came in after midnight, drinking.

—Floyd came in late and stayed about 30 minutes. I followed him to his office to talk to him. He would not see me. I broke the glass door knocking.

—Floyd came by and got another suit of clothes and left again, to be back Friday. Police were here tonight looking for Floyd.

—I went to police station to try to pay Floyd's checks off. They would not let me do it.

—Floyd called me tonight at Virginia's (a neighbor). First time I had talked to him since he left here 18 days earlier. He said he was not working with Jack after tomorrow and he said he is leaving the country. Wants me to store our furniture because he says he can't pay the rent. Floyd says he has 19 warrants against him in Oak Ridge I didn't know about.

—I've been lying awake a lot throughout the night. I'm thinking and dreading divorce. I seem to be able to see no other way. We do not know where Floyd is. Do not know where he's staying.

As always, Mother never let on that she was having sleepless nights. She made sure my brothers and I focused on school and the responsibilities that we had. My brother, Gee, was a really good kid and very protective of me in high school. Growing up, I picked on Gee a lot, but he was never allowed to get back at me. "Boys do not hit girls," Mother would always say. In high school, Gee would critique any boy that I dated. Like Mother, he was an avid reader, devouring every book he could get his hands on. When I moved to Atlanta at age eighteen, Gee decided to move there as well, and for a while we shared an apartment. One day, he was crossing Peachtree Street in the Brookhaven area of Atlanta when a gentleman approached him. "Young man," the person said, "by any chance are you looking for a job?" Gee answered in the affirmative and the man hired him on the spot to wear tuxedos for a fashion catalog. My brother was very handsome pictured in his tuxedo.

Within a year or so, Gee moved back to Tennessee and enrolled in college where he was very serious about his studies. He met his wife after graduation and they have one son. Gee later made mission trips to Russia and England, serving as an overseas lectureship director. He has edited and published books and has recently become a patent holder. Today, he works with an internet advertising firm and everyone knows Gee as Gary. We are still very close and being just thirteen months apart, we have endured so much together. Growing up, we had to laugh just to keep from crying. Today, Gary still makes me laugh and laugh and laugh.

As my baby brother John Chris got older, he grew less

and less fragile and we all became accustomed to his condition. With Mother's encouragement, he became a participant in a self-help group for children with epilepsy in Oak Ridge. He never wanted us to describe his condition as epilepsy, instead he told us he had a "seizure disorder." Understandably, he did not want to be referred to as someone with a disability. "Everybody deals with something," John Chris would say, "I happen to deal with a seizure disorder." He was exactly right.

My brother loved to play the drums as a kid. He would constantly be drumming with sticks, straws, chopsticks and pencils…anything he could get his hands on. He drummed on table tops, he drummed on furniture and he drummed all the time. He drove us all nuts, especially Mother! Elaine bought him a single drum when he was about 10 years old and later John Chris obtained a complete drum set at a garage sale. Drumming was his world.

When John Chris was sixteen, he started hanging around with a group of teenagers who were experimenting with drugs. The drug scene was completely foreign to Mother. She was as pure as the driven snow and none of her other children had gone down that road. The decision was made for John Chris to leave high school early and move to Atlanta in hopes of getting him away from the crowd he was associating with. I was barely twenty-two when he moved to Atlanta. When he arrived, his red hair hung in his eyes and it had grown down to his shoulders. He first worked in a temporary construction job and then flipped burgers at a hamburger joint for a while. I think because he had not finished high school, his self-esteem had sunk low.

Eventually, he was given the opportunity to apprentice as a dental laboratory technician where he mastered the art of "waxing" dental crowns and bridges. Over a thirty year period, he held two jobs in dental laboratories in Atlanta. He was a loyal employee, seldom missing a day of work. John Chris frequently had seizures which caused him to lose touch with reality for an instant, and then he would go about his work without missing a beat. What drove John Chris was not praise or a huge salary. Instead, he was content to have a nice job to go to every day, and to be able to work comfortably within the limitations of his disorder. John Chris married a nice, young woman who was a fellow student of mine at nursing school, and they raised two boys in Atlanta.

John Chris endured his seizure disorder with much more grace than I ever could have. Even though he could drop to the floor with a grand mal seizure at any given time, he never considered himself as someone having a disability. Perhaps he practiced Mother's philosophy of "rising above" more than the rest of us. In 2007, John Chris underwent major brain surgery. Dr. David Olsen, the neurologist treating John Chris, suggested my brother was a candidate for a newer surgery which was thought to lesson seizures in an epileptic patient. I admire Dr. Olsen for thinking "outside the box" where my baby brother was concerned. John Chris was evaluated at Emory University Hospital in Atlanta and scheduled for an amygliohypocampectomy. There were many risks involved in this eleven-hour brain surgery, but John

Chris was willing to do anything for a better quality of life.

Mother was skeptical and voiced her fears. She accompanied John Chris and myself to Emory for his pre-operative appointment. The intake nurse at Emory took us to a private room and began asking questions. "John, where were you born?" she asked. After he answered, she exclaimed, "I am from Oak Ridge, too. My name is Anne Bigelow, my father is Robert Bigelow." Well, there you have it, if the daughter of Dr. Bigelow was a part of this process, then everything was going to be OK! At least, that was Mother's reasoning.

And everything was OK. The surgery was a success and at age 49, my baby brother was seizure free. John Chris had entered a whole new world.

{ Twenty Five }

VIKING ROAD, 1970

IT OCCURRED TO me as a teenager that when you move multiple times, sometimes returning to the same street and sometimes to the same house, these may be signs you are moving too often. When I was six years old, we lived on Viking Road in Oak Ridge (the apartment where Gee and I put Monkeyface, the cat, in the clothes dryer). At age eighteen, we moved to the apartment right next door! It was strange to have some of the same neighbors and the same yard. If we had owned an automobile, we would have had the same parking space! The best part was that my sister, Elaine, and her family lived right next door.

I was in my senior year in high school with graduation approaching soon. It was embarrassing to move from house to house so frequently and navigating through school was extremely difficult. I had to borrow school supplies constantly. I was still working at Western Auto after school and on Saturdays to try to help Mother with finances. She was crocheting a lot of ladies' ponchos and caps, which were popular at that time. They sold for $10.00 per set.

But suddenly, things were not going well for Mother. She was told she needed immediate surgery for possible uterine cancer.

—I went to Dr. Pugh for a check-up. Found high blood pressure, a temperature and he found a fibroid tumor. Took a pap smear.

—Had surgery today. Dr. Pugh says everything went like he had expected. Elaine, Paula and Floyd have stayed all day. Merle and Linda came tonight.

—I definitely have cancer.

Nezzie Allen went with her to the hospital the day of her surgery. Mother instructed Gee and I to stay at home with John Chris, who was almost twelve years old. Nezzie stayed by Mother's side to comfort her and see to her every need. When the surgery was over, we were relieved to learn the cancer was confined to Mother's cervix. I never saw a pathology report, but we were told the cancer was removed completely. At the time, we really did not understand the magnitude of this positive report: Mother was cancer free. The worst side effect was the utter terror which remained with Mother. For the rest of her life, she feared the cancer would return. As any cancer survivor will attest, the least little twinge of pain makes a person tremble. However, Mother usually kept her fears to herself so as not to worry us.

A few days after high school graduation, I bought a Greyhound Bus ticket for my trip to Atlanta, where I moved to further my education. I was 18 years old. My long-term plan was to complete a medical assisting training program, get a job, and then work my way through nursing school. My first years away from home were rather busy, and I was experiencing new adventures every day. To say I was naïve is a huge understatement. I did a lot of silly things, such as riding an express city bus which took me miles past my designated stop. Still, Atlanta was my new home. Clearly, the city was a big change from east Tennessee.

I fared well in the MA program, making top marks. After graduation, I was hired to *teach* medical assisting in the evenings for $5 per hour. Luckily, I got a job in a doctor's office right away, working for a pulmonologist named Dr. Walter Dunbar. I was a sponge, learning everything I could as I worked in his medical practice. Verion Ross, a lady who had worked with Dr. Dunbar for over thirty years, soon became a friend and mentor. She trusted me enough to co-sign a loan permitting me to purchase my first car. It was a used, red convertible Volkswagen Beetle, which cost $450. I missed my family back in Tennessee. The only form of communication was the postal service. I wrote to Mother often and she wrote to me almost every day. Neither of us had a telephone.

Without a shadow of a doubt, I thought I had grown up in the happiest surroundings in the world in Tennessee. I considered myself fortunate to have over sixty first cousins, a huge extended family, and siblings who I loved dearly. It never occurred to me it was not normal to move twenty-five times in eighteen years. We just did the best we could, rising above whatever circumstances we found ourselves in.

—*Received a card in the mail from Mo and Linda with a twenty-dollar bill enclosed for grocery money.*

—*Gee left today to catch a ride to Atlanta. Left his money here for me to use for rent. Paula sent some, too. I paid rent and deposit and got the house key today. Gee left hitch-hiking. I'm so worried about him tonight. My children are the best in the world. I am so thankful for them.*

—*Last night was the first I've ever spent alone.*

Within a few years after I left Tennessee, Mother was an empty-nester. Gee had moved out and John Chris had come to Atlanta. So, Mother landed a sales job at Proffit's Department Store in Oak Ridge, selling men's high-end clothing. She was thrilled to buy her sons clothes with her 20% discount. Mother worked there for ten years or more and was honored as "Sales Clerk of the Year" many times. She enjoyed the commissions she earned, most of all.

When my Grizzell grandparents passed away, my aunts and uncles made a wise business decision to subdivide the Grizzell Farm. In doing this, they were able sell the land for the highest possible market value and divide the proceeds among the nine children, which included the family of my late Uncle John Pope Grizzell. For my father's portion, they first deducted all of the monies my father owed to the family and to my late grandparents. I have no idea what my father's total share of the inheritance would have been, but eleven thousand dollars was what remained. His siblings thought so highly of Mother, they gave her his Grizzell inheritance. My father never saw the eleven thousand dollars. Mother bought a nice automobile, the first car she ever had, with some of the money. She paid cash for a slightly-used, olive green Pontiac. She also now enjoyed excellent credit, which was very important to her. Mother could cash a check anywhere in town without showing identification. She was one happy lady!

In fact, it would be inaccurate to describe Mother as ever being *unhappy*, for she found true joy in life's most basic things. Even when times were tough, she did the best she could without dwelling on situations she could not remedy. She was content with her friends, family and faith. And, now that she had transportation, she could visit family as often as she pleased. Many times, she drove to Florida to visit Mo and his family or came to Atlanta to visit John Chris and myself. Gee had settled in middle Tennessee, and she loved going to his house, too. Elaine was the only one of Mother's five children who resided close to Oak Ridge and the two of them were especially close.

Mother was present for the birth of all ten of her grandchildren. When she wasn't visiting us, we visited her as often as we could. Later in life, she was especially fond of seeing her eight great-grandchildren, who called Mother "GG." Interestingly, I know people today who visit their parents out of sheer obligation, but visiting our mother was always fun. We all truly enjoyed her. She was the cornerstone of our family.

In the early 1980s, Mother had finally arrived. She was hired at the atomic energy plant in Oak Ridge. She worked at

K-25 as a janitor, which she considered to be a very prestigious job. She had access to every single inch of the plant and felt empowered as very few jobs there had that kind of security clearance. She wore a dosimeter every day to measure the amount of radiation she was exposed to. She worked around centrifuges and containers which housed radiation, plutonium, beryllium, mercury and uranium. The fact that she saw and heard secretive data, which Mother took an oath never to discuss, made her very proud. And trust me, she never did share. Nobody could keep a secret like my mother. She worked the evening shift which suited her well. Living alone, she could return home before midnight, watch *The Johnny Carson Show* and sleep as late as she wanted the next morning.

Mother had witnessed the cancer diagnosis of many who worked in and around K-25 and the other nuclear energy plants, including the illness of my Uncle John Pope. The possibility of dangerous exposure to the materials housed at the plants was enough to frighten anybody. However, it was the chance people took when they moved to the "Atomic City." My mother, herself a cancer survivor, took that chance. The job opportunities were endless and the salaries were unprecedented at a time when employment was hard to find. I have no knowledge if the dosimeter Mother wore ever revealed dangerous levels of radiation. I have no knowledge if she was ever exposed to the elements she worked around every day. However, from what I understand, there was a spill or accident of some kind during one of the early years Mother was employed at the plant. Because our mother eventually did die of cancer, the US Department of Labor compensated our family financially shortly after her passing.

Mother last saw my father when he visited at the hospital where she was recovering from cancer surgery in 1970. After he walked out of that hospital room, she expected him to come strolling home at some point, as he had done from time to time before. But, he did not stroll home and many years passed. She knew he was alive and well, due to reports from his siblings. Then one day, she heard he had another family in Bristol, Tennessee, over one hundred miles from Oak Ridge.

All her life, my mother believed in the sanctity of marriage. For her, divorce was never an option. But now, after so many years of estrangement, this was different. "I think I will go and get myself a divorce!" Mother said. She marched to the Anderson County courthouse and soon obtained an uncontested dissolution of the marriage, which did not even require my father's signature. As difficult as this was for her to do, she was at peace knowing she had done the right thing. Mother was finally free of debt, worry and indecision. And she was finally free of my father.

After remaining on Viking Road for another decade, Mother would live only in two more places the next thirty years of her life. She leased a one-bedroom duplex on Outer Drive in Oak Ridge for fifteen years. The apartment was clean, had a nice yard, and was across the street from her friend, Dora Forrest. Mother and Nezzie Allen remained the best of friends, never suspecting they would share grandchildren one day. Mother and Agnes Hogg had an added surprise when their grandchildren, who lived in Atlanta, became best friends. Mother and Agnes continued to make one Sugar Lump doll after another. Mother, Agnes, Dora and Nezzie connected in many ways and were always there for each other. They were quite a foursome!

Mother would be the first of her friends to pass away in 2008 at age 80. She was diagnosed with a rare form of lymphoma and she left us quickly. She came to Northside Hospital in Atlanta for treatment, but she was gone in only three weeks. We will always be grateful for the kindness shown by the wonderful oncologist, Steve Szabo, MD, and the healthcare workers at Northside. Dr. Szabo was instrumental in helping Mother face her disease and arranged for hospice care at my home in Atlanta. Mother spent her final days with a calm and peaceful resolve. Mo coordinated a beautiful funeral service that celebrated and praised Mother's life. Gee led us all in singing a few of Mother's favorite spirituals. Two of her grandsons led prayers. We were all heart-broken.

Her final resting place is Sycamore, Tennessee, where many in Mother's family are buried. Prior to her death, her last fifteen years in Oak Ridge were spent in the nicest home she ever had. My husband, Tom, bought a "B" house for her off Michigan Avenue in the early 1990s. The house was high on a hilltop and had a perfect white picket fence, which had been erected by her sons and grandsons.

The house was toasty warm in the winter and cool in the summer, which may not sound like a big deal, but to Mother it was. Until then, she had never had air conditioning. Mother had her own bedroom and her own bed, and it was a real bed, too, not a fold-out cot. She had her own chest of drawers, her own furniture, her own TV and her own phone. She had a washer and a dryer, and of course, a sewing machine. She had electricity and hot running water. She had a refrigerator stocked with food and a car sitting in her driveway. Mother now had the conveniences of life to add to the wealth of love she always shared with her family.

And so goes the story of my mother.

Epilogue

My dear brother, John Chris, died in his sleep in 2010. After my brother's brain surgery, a whole new world had opened up for him. For almost three years, he had been seizure free. John Chris left a permanent mark in the hearts of his siblings and children; there will never be anyone quite like him. He is buried in Sycamore, Tennessee, beside Mother.

When the mourners were departing from the funeral, a recording of my brother's favorite song, *Tears In Heaven* by Eric Clapton, was played. The service was a traditional southern funeral, where those who wanted to say goodbye to John Chris could do so at his coffin. Just before the lid was closed and sealed, one of John Chris' sons pulled his father's drumsticks from his jacket and tossed them into the coffin. "Dad and his drumsticks," he smiled, "they'll be driving Grandmother crazy for the next one hundred years."

My father came to John Chris' funeral. It was the first time he ever saw the majority of his grandchildren and great-grandchildren. It had been forty years since he left our family and, at the funeral, he told us he'd like to do better. I hoped that he meant it.

My brother, Mo, recently wrote and published a beautiful song, emphasizing the affection we all shared for our mother. What a fitting way to draw this story to a close.

Five Thimbles (the song)

She was taken by his smile,
a heart so young and tender.
wouldn't know 'til five kids later,
the hurt that love would render.

A life of pain and heartache,
left to make it on her own.
No place to live, five mouths to feed,
she never felt so all alone.

But there were five shiny thimbles,
to make little shirts and skirts.
With scraps and rags discarded,
for Sunday's walk to church.
For Sunday's walk to church.

Pride she could not afford,
unless it was in her five.
Working for little at anything,
so they could all survive.

Never thinking of herself,
never a store bought dress.
Never a dinner out,
always self-less-ness.

> *And there were five worn out thimbles,*
> *things to make and things to sell.*
> *Working, struggling night and day,*
> *'cept for God, no one to tell.*
> *'cept for God, no one to tell*

'neath tough determination,
Lay a fragile, loved crushed soul.
The only love of her life,
would never be coming home.

Thought it couldn't get harder,
but when her youngest nearly died,
she was looking up at rock bottom,
seemed nothing to do but cry.

> *But there were five tarnished thimbles,*
> *stained with sweat and tears.*
> *"Rise above your situation",*
> *a motto lived all her years.*
> *A motto lived all her years.*

The center of love and affection,
now grandkids and family all.
Finally time to be with,
the little faces on her wall.

But the end came so quickly,
so many hearts left with a hole.
No big estate to leave,
she left her heart and soul.

And there were five precious thimbles,
found among her things.
Leaving the perfect treasure,
inheritance fit for kings.
Inheritance fit for kings.

Now there are five golden thimbles,
up in heav's fair land.
Sowing the love of a mother,
waiting with outstretched hands.
Waiting with outstretched hands.

The End.

About the author

Paula Grizzell DeMarini lives with her husband in Atlanta, Georgia, and has two children. She has worked as a chemotherapist and pharmaceutical sales representative and is currently a physician liaison at a leading Atlanta hospital. Her husband is a physician in pulmonary and critical care medicine. This is her first published book.

Photograph by Robin Gaucher

To learn which booksellers
currently are carrying
Five Thimbles,
please visit our website,
www.fivethimbles.com
Thank you.

CPSIA information can be obtained at www.ICGtesting.com
Printed in the USA
LVOW040036250212

270301LV00003B/4/P